CONTENTS

Contents

VOICES AND INSTRUMENTS

Avril Dankworth

Illustrations by Leslie Priestley

HART-DAVIS
EDUCATIONAL

This book is dedicated to Miss Frances Knowles, the staff and children of Lionel Road School, Brentford, Middlesex.

Granada Publishing Limited
Published by Hart-Davis Educational Ltd
Frogmore, St. Albans, Hertfordshire
First Published 1973
Second Impression 1978

Copyright © 1973 by Avril Dankworth

ISBN 0 247 12513 X
0020472
Printed in Great Britain by
Fletcher & Son Ltd, Norwich

FOREWORD

To most people music means re-creation of a printed score, but recently a great deal of experiment has been made in the extemporisation and composition of music.

No teacher who experiments with voices and instruments —whether his involvement be complete or only partial —can work without at least a nodding acquaintance with the work of Carl Orff. Movement, percussion bands and recorder work flourished in England in many schools before the second world war; but it is surely to Carl Orff that we owe the everspreading use of simple instruments (especially pitch percussion) in the classroom.

These are used in various ways, linked with art, poetry, song and movement, but again the interest in truly creative work as class and group activity has gained in popularity with Carl Orff's ideas built upon the use of speech patterns and the pentatonic scale as a starting-point. The school music broadcasts on radio and television continually bring further ideas to encourage and inspire group music-making with voices and instruments.

This book sets out to show how simple and effective musical activities may be introduced into the classroom by using rhythm and melody instruments for the pleasure of creating accompaniments, songs and instrumental pieces in a spirit of spontaneity; used imaginatively these instruments can invigorate any music lesson and provide opportunity for creative music activity, the work being linked with ear and eye training, leading directly to the reading of scores and parts. Much of the work is based upon traditional rather than twentieth-century techniques.

It is becoming more generally realised that this type of work is by no means limited to the primary school, and that, adequately developed, it can play a valuable and even essential part at all stages of a child's development. With the prospect of more leisure in adult life, the involvement of music-making in all its forms has a tremendously important part to play.

Activity and discovery are as vital and essential in music as they are in art, science and mathematics. By incorporating instruments into the general classroom work we stand more possibility of involving everyone in the class at some point of our work, because we can provide for every level of interest, ability and imagination; our resources are widened to a degree that the singing lesson on its own can never achieve.

Music is the most social of subjects, reliant as it is upon individual responsibility contributing towards the whole effect. This is particularly significant in the involvement of boys, whose first interest in music is often instrumental rather than vocal; capture their interest by means of activity and discovery in the primary school, and their continued interest at secondary level will thus avoid the regrets of many musical teenage boys that they didn't learn sooner to play an instrument and read music.

In this book there is no actual 'scheme of work'; the ideas suggested here provide a basis which can be adapted to any age-group, the teacher acting as a guide to the children's various activities and discoveries. For every teacher handling an unconventional approach, the most important qualities are enthusiasm and initiative, which will override fears and disappointments and bring courage to explore new territory. For this reason some of the best results can often come not from the music specialist but from enthusiastic general practitioners who know their children and encourage originality. Not all good musicians have these gifts.

Ideally the music syllabus should embrace singing, movement, playing, listening and notation work; interwoven into this pattern must be a balance of involvement in re-creative music-making and creative work in the form of extemporisation and composition of music. No-one teaches English or a foreign language without balancing three approaches:

1 creative work–oral and written composition, which is self-expression of thoughts and ideas,

2 reading,

and

3 appreciation and re-creation of poetry, literature and drama.

Since music is a language, a similar balance should exist, time not being grudged for creative work. A baby learns his native language by hearing and speaking it and *much later* he learns to read, write and appreciate literature. Surely then, it is illogical to use the conventional —and often formal —method of presenting music symbols before children have experienced the language of music.

Further, it is when a child orally invents a story that his desire to record it makes writing a necessity; it is when he enjoys listening to stories and poems that he desires to read for himself. And so musically: the foundations can be laid without any reference to symbols. The enjoyment of re-creative and creative singing and playing leads to the child's desire to read and write music, in order to be independent.

INTRODUCTION

Much of the work involving voices and instruments in the classroom is concerned with accompaniment; once a melodic line is known (be it vocal or instrumental) it is possible to try the children with some form of accompaniment to give more rhythmic drive and colour, 'dressing-up' or 'backing' the melodic line. Decisions have to be made about the effects and the rhythmic detail: at first the teacher chooses these, then hands over to the children, but as soon as possible the children themselves take the initiative.

The effects available for accompaniment are:

1 rhythm sounds of no definite pitch,

2 melody sounds of definite pitch,

or, of course, a combination of the two, chosen for their suitability to the style or topic of the music.

The detailed content may be:

1 improvised (composed spontaneously at the time of performance),

2 formal (consciously incorporating 'basic' principles of rhythm, melody and harmony),

3 read from a score,

or a mixture of these. The accompaniment must never detract from the melody, so the emphasis must always be on listening to:

1 the suitability of choice of effects and detailed content

2 the balance of melody and accompaniment

3 the general ensemble.

The melodic line may be extant or it may be an original tune composed by someone in the group. Therefore this book has been planned in two sections:

I. Accompaniment of existing vocal and instrumental material

II. Further developments and application of these ideas to children's original work.

These two sections of the book can be worked together and are not necessarily in order of use; rhythmic ideas come first because rhythmic consciousness is basic to everything.

MUSIC CORNER

In both infant and junior departments it is becoming more and more customary to find a music corner as one of the activities available for children when their class is divided for group and individual work. Here is the opportunity for children to follow up the work begun in their class music lesson and to prepare for future sessions. Here should be made available some or all of the instruments used, so that the children may practise the technique of holding and playing the instruments; practise, copy and write music; invent rhythms and melodies and generally experiment with sounds and symbols.

Books on instruments, books of songs and books about music should all be available for the children. Opportunities should also be given for them to make stories, pictures, scrapbooks and models connected with, or inspired by, music; and, of course if possible, a record-player made available with a collection of records — and even a small tape-recorder.

PART I

Accompaniment for existing vocal and instrumental material

PART I

The material to be accompanied

There is a wide variety of music suitable for this type of work, particularly songs and instrumental pieces with dancelike rhythms. Many folk songs sound far more natural accompanied by simple classroom instruments in preference to the piano. Spanish, North and South American and Central European songs lend themselves particularly well to Latin-American type of accompaniment. Minstrel songs, spirituals and sea shanties seem to have a special attraction for the 11 to 18 age group. Strong rhythm and lilting melody are the vital elements of appeal.

It is important to choose music which offers a good variety of styles and tempi and gives scope for selection of suitable accompanying material. The teacher must also choose music which helps the children to develop awareness of dynamic levels, with every colour from pp to ff, ⟨ (crescendo) and ⟩ (diminuendo), according to the type of music and the word-content in each verse of a song.

For detailed list of material see Appendix 2.

1 RHYTHM ACCOMPANIMENT

Effects

Effects available

The effects available involve sounds of no definite pitch; these are:
  i Body sounds
 ii Mouth music
iii Rhythm instruments

i Body sounds

These consist of four sounds made with hands and feet (always readily available) and known by the children as 'snap, crackle, pop, bang':

a) finger clicks
if the children cannot produce a sound, they mime and click the tongue instead.

b) hand claps
there are three kinds: 1) when rounded palms, producing a 'hearty applause' clap, 2) with flat fingers and palms which gives a dry slappy sound and 3) fingers only for very light texture.

c) knee slaps
keep loose wrists and flap the hands on the thighs with a bouncing action. A useful effect in itself, the movement is excellent practice for playing bongoes and maracas.

d) footstamps and toe taps
—may be performed by either using one foot repeatedly or by alternating the two feet. Toe taps are sometimes preferable for giving variety of volume.

ii Mouth music (including whistling)

The voice is used virtually as an instrument, producing short and long consonants, sung or spoken vowels and diphthongs and 'comic-paper' words; these may be used in their own right or for producing sound effects.

e.g. tongue clicks	for horses' hooves
sh.............	for waves
oo—oo—oo	for ghosts and wind
z—z—z	for machinery
ah	for a falling rocket
boom	for an explosion

iii **Rhythm instruments**

Rhythm instruments include the standard orchestral and the Latin-American percussion instruments. Naturally, quality varies, but it pays to buy the best and there is available a series of booklets published by the British Standards Institute *Specifications for School Music Equipment*, available from British Standards House, 2 Park Street, London W1. Homemade instruments may be used to augment the number of instruments available, to supplement the sound effects required and as an introduction to good quality authentic instruments.

There are six main classes of rhythm instruments:

a) drum
a stretched membrane (head) over a hollow cylinder (body)

b) gong
a suspended body which vibrates when struck with a stick

  bell
a gong with its stick attached loosely inside

c) jingles
little pieces of material which jingle against each other when moved

d) shaker
a container with contents which rattle against the sides of the container when shaken

e) clappers
two like surfaces clapped together

f) scraper
anything with a ridged surface which can be scraped

	Orchestral	**Latin-American**	**Additional effects**
drum	sidedrum	finger drums 2 small bongoes large conga	tom tom bassdrum
gong	single cymbal triangle	cowbell hit with stick	tap box chinese block gong
jingles	tambourine	tambourine	jingle stick jingle bells
shaker		chocolo maracas	
clappers	pair cymbals castanets	claves	whip indian bells
scraper		guiro	

Homemade rhythm instruments

Just as primitive man utilised the objects he found around him in the jungle for producing sound, so we can put to good use many things that come to hand in the kitchen, garage and gardening shed. Be sure that homemade instruments are really strong, otherwise much time can be wasted on repairs and replacements. Provided that they sound effective there is no need to be apologetic or snobbish about using them.

a) drum

The membrane may be of leather, rubber, plastic or several layers of greaseproof paper and butter muslin (or net curtain) stuck together with size. Stretch the membrane over the tin, flowerpot or cylinder and secure it with a) glue, b) string, wire or thick rubber bands like a jam jar covering, c) nails or d) string lacing from top to bottom through a curtain ring. There are more ambitious and time-consuming ways of making drums, but the above method is quick and effective.

    The tight-fitting plastic lids on coffee tins and plastic food-containers make instant stretched membranes; the base of the latter also makes an acceptable light sound, though it is not a stretched membrane.

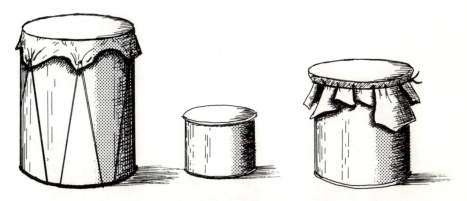

Collect as many different shapes, sizes and heads of drum as possible. These are generally used as finger (bongo) drums, but drumsticks are essential for variety of effect. They may be made from a) hardwood balls attached to dowel rod, b) thin bamboo bound with rubber bands at one end, c) spoons padded with cotton–wool — giving hard, medium or soft beaters. d) Brushes are also useful for special effects.

b) gong

A flowerpot makes an excellent gong. It may be suspended by a cotton reel or nail on a piece of string, a knotted rope or a bent wire; or a glockenspiel beater.

It is possible to play melodies from a set of carefully selected flowerpots; the pitch can be flattened by sticking a knob of putty inside the rim of the flowerpot.

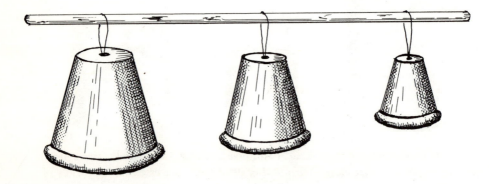

The knob-end of a shoe-tree makes a very successful gongstick; play on the rim of the pot.

Other suspended bodies:

block of hard wood	large metal washer
metal tube or bar	tin lid
horseshoe	iron frying pan

Experiment with the various effects obtainable from hard, medium or soft gongsticks.

c) jingles
These can be made from curtain rings, bottle-tops, buttons, beads, nutshells. They may be strung together on a string or wire loop or mounted on a stick.

jinglestick
Lay the bottletops with the teeth upwards, flatten them with a hammer and make a large hole in the middle of each. Mount them with screws or nails on to a wooden stick, all to one end.

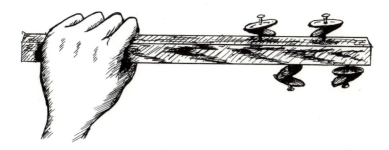

When playing, one hand grasps the free end of the stick and the other taps on the space between the hand and the jingles; be sure that the screws are vertical and not lying horizontally. Another way of playing is to 'trill' (i.e. tremble) the instrument like a tambourine, which is, of course, a jingle-drum.

jingle bells
A very successful effect comes from metal filmspools strung together in pairs.

d) shaker
Container of wood, tin, plastic, cardboard with small contents: rice, pearl barley, spaghetti pieces, tiny beads, buttons, stones, fruit pips, fruit stones. Do not overfill.

chocolo
A long tube-shape container: Metal or cardboard tubing, plastic container, long biscuit tin, or two short tins sellotaped together (shown on next page).

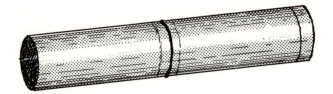

To play, grasp the two ends of the instrument, holding it horizontally, then shake in front of the body, forwards and backwards, up and down, side to side, etc. For detailed rhythms, hold the chocolo vertically, so that the contents lie in the base of the tube; gently support the top end and put all energy into the other hand, working loosely from the wrist.

maracas
Shakers with handles, usually played in pairs; the left hand one may contain slightly heavier filling than the right, thus producing a slightly different effect.

plastic bouncing balls
Pierce and add filling, then insert handle, push through the ball and catch with a screw on the opposite side.

plastic skittles are useful as maracas
Pierce a small hole in the base with the scissor point, then push each grain of rice separately through the hole into the skittle.

ballcock
Drill a hole through the top, insert the filling, then bang in a tapered piece of wood to make the handle.

Play maracas with a flick of the wrist; practise by bouncing the maracas on the knee, then lift away, maintaining the same movement. This gives a definite, crisp effect rather than an indeterminate rattle. Shakers may also be effectively 'trilled' like jingles.

e) clappers
Metal tins, cardboard boxes, bones, woodblocks, stones, sticks.

claves
Two thick hardwood sticks. Six-inch lengths of broom-handle make excellent claves.
Hold the lefthand stick very loosely or even lay it across the fingernails, leaving a
little pocket of air beneath, which acts as a resonator to the vibrations.

Bounce the right hand clave on to the left hand one, producing a ringing sound; this
cannot happen if the sticks are grasped tightly.

whip
Two hinged slats of wood, each 30 by 5 cm. Crack them together smartly.

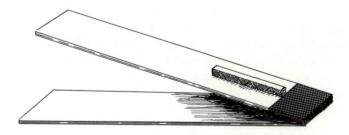

f) scraper
Washboard, corrugated cardboard, ridged pelmet board, comb, sandpaper blocks.

guiro or resi-resi
A fifteen centimetre length of wide bamboo cut with notches about 2 cm apart.

Scrape with metal, plastic or wooden stick; each gives a different effect.

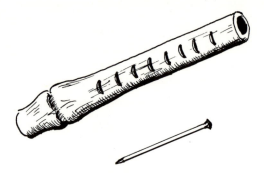

bullroarer
A slat of plywood about 5 by 15 cm with a few perforations on a yard of strong string.

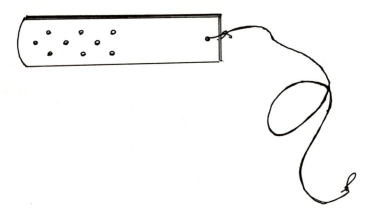

Hold the end of the string in one hand and turn the wood at the other end until the string becomes twisted; then twirl the slat like a windmill.

This instrument is used in Africa by the witchdoctors to frighten away evil spirits. The sound is a roaring one, and hence its name. The evil spirits think that a real bull is giving chase, so they flee the village, then all sick people recover!

A safer form of bullroarer is made with a circle of cardboard on a ring of string threaded through two holes.

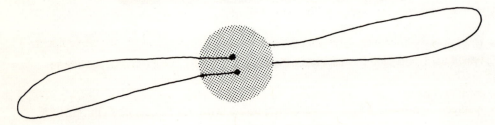

All these instruments may be made in a size suitable for the performers, and decorated in bright colours; they are easy to play and do not demand a very advanced technique. The sound they make has a genuine Latin-American flavour which is colourful and attractive; moreover, the instruments are familiar to the children, for they see them on film and television.

Links with other subjects

The work of making the instruments may well be linked with the 'science of sound', although the actual construction and decoration may be done as handicraft and art activity. Children enjoy inventing and making their own instruments, and often the project stimulates interest in all kinds of instruments; exotic examples from many parts of the world arrive at school and their geographical sources have to be traced. Links between music and language develop as the instruments are put into use for dramatic sound effect and speech rhythms. They may also be used in movement and dance.

Choice of effects

The effects must be related to the style and topic of the music, and may be selected for their dramatic sound effect value.

Certain national music evokes the use of particular effects:
Spain tambourines, castanets, handclaps, finger clicks, footstamps
Latin-America complete set of Latin-American instruments
Africa drums, knee slaps and handclaps
Austria all four body sounds as used in *Schuhplattler* dancing

Certain moods of music suggest the suitable choice of accompanying effects:
lullaby shaker and jingles
loud, fast-moving music drums, gongs, clappers, four body sounds
lilting music shakers, jingles and scrapers

Many songs evoke an accompaniment of dramatic sound effects: Here are some examples, marked to indicate their age-suitability:

i) Songs about soldiers, drummer boys and drums demand a drum accompaniment:

(infant)   a) **Tin Soldiers** *Activity Songs for the Nursery*, Dainton (Paxton)

(junior)   b) **Three Drummer Boys** *French folksong (Sheet)* (OUP)

(senior)   c) **The Gentlemen Soldiers** *Penguin Folksong Book*

ii) Gongs can be used for clocks chiming or bells ringing, especially in Christmas music:

(infant)	a)	**Tinkle, tinkle** *Play Songs*, Southam (Feldman)
(junior/senior)	b)	**Farewell to the old year** *Music for Children, I* (Schott)
(junior/senior)	c)	**The Christmas bells are ringing** *Israeli round (sheet)* (Chappell)

iii) Shakers produce an effective storm in:

(infant)	a)	**Pray open your umbrella** *Fingers and Thumbs*, Elliot (Stainer & Bell/Galliard)
(junior)	b)	**Old Mister Noah** Perry *(sheet)* (OUP)

and any other songs about Noah and the ark, or the sound of waves washing the shore for:

(infant)	a)	**The sea, the wavy sea** *New Nursery Jingles*, Barnard (Curwen)
(junior/senior)	b)	**My bonnie lies over the ocean**

and any sea shanties or ballads.

iv) Clappers can be used together with jingles for horses galloping in:

(infant)	a)	**Rocking horse** *Play Songs*, Southam (Feldman)
(junior/senior)	b)	**Jim, the carter lad** *Dorset folksong (sheet)* (Curwen)
	c)	**Cowboy songs**

and also for the clock ticking in clock songs:

(infant)	a)	**Tick tock** *Play Songs*, Southam (Feldman)
(junior)	b)	**Clock carol** *Sing Round the year*, Swann (Bodley Head)
(junior/senior)	c)	**Grandfather's clock** *Something to Sing*, Book I (CUP)

v) Scrapers give the sounds of ducks quacking in:

(infant)	a)	**The yellow duck** *Toycupboard Songs*, Rees (Novello)
	b)	**Farmyard Songs**

and also make effective machinery sounds (together with shakers and clappers and mouth music 'z—z—z—z') for songs like:

(infant/junior)	a)	**The mill wheel** *Thirty Folk Settings for Children* (Curwen)
(junior/senior)	b)	**The Manx spinning song** *(sheet)* (YBP/Chappell)
(senior)	c)	**Dirty old town** *Something to Sing Book I* (CUP)

Dramatic sound effects

Teachers who are modest about their ability as singers may well find this kind of work a useful extension of the music lesson as such, music overspilling into language, the aim being to develop an awareness of sound quality and quantity. Bearing in mind the effects available (body sounds, mouth music, instruments), songs, poems, stories, plays and pictures are chosen for their possibility of interpolating dramatic sound effects. This is an opportunity for the children to imitate familiar sounds in dramatic situations.

With the younger children it is obvious to add movement to the accompanied song wherever possible. Some children coordinate all three activities of sing, play, and move; others prefer to accept responsibility for only one or two.

At first the teacher will have to guide the choice of instruments, but very quickly the children will make the suggestions. It is useful to compile lists of songs, poems, stories and plays which lend themselves to this kind of treatment.

The links between music and language are infinite: poems may often be happily used as interludes between verses of a song—or vice versa.

Once the instruments have been introduced and the idea of accompaniment is familiar to the children, introductions, interludes and postludes to the songs may be improvised. When the class is reasonably experienced, the children can make their own arrangements, then come forward to lead the class. This work may, of course, be combined with melody instruments, also chosen for their suitability to a particular song.

See PART II for further developments.

Detailed content

Improvisation

From the start the children should be given an opportunity to improvise rhythms for themselves, each participating at his own level of ability. One of the quickest ways to get a group improvising is by the use of a record player; the children can concentrate entirely on their improvisation, while the teacher is free to organise and assist. The teacher chooses a recording of music with good rhythm and catchy melody then asks the players to slap the knees slowly, quickly and very quickly while the music is in progress. At first, the teacher directs the changes, but soon each player works on his own; the music stimulates the improvisation, and is itself made more colourful by the accompaniment. The next step is to add the other body sounds, then incorporate rhythm instruments —first bongoes and maracas, then the other four types.

For variety, divide the class into two, four and six groups, and get each to improvise when indicated by the teacher; children can also take a turn at leading. A group may be of miscellaneous instruments or all of similar ilk, i.e. drum group, shaker group, etc. The experience in improvisation thus gained can be transferred to accompany singing or developed as a means of listening.

Improvisation —to accompany songs

It is a good idea to let improvisation to records and songs go hand in hand. In themselves recordings of folksongs are a useful accompaniment to children's voices as an alternative to live accompaniment. They can also be very useful in encouraging the participating singers to play at the same time (they can dance, too), this dual activity being continued independently when the recorded music is faded out.

Folk dance records can set the mood and style for the song to be accompanied afterwards; improvisation to the recorded music gets the players into practice for the song.

Once the idea of improvisation has been established it isn't, of course, necessary to warm up the players in this way every time; the spirit of a song is caught immediately and suitable effects discussed and decided.

Improvisation —as a means of listening

i) *Movement of some kind* is the most natural reponse to music. Just as children enjoy playing an instrument, so they enjoy using the body to accompany music, moving quite freely. The most simple response is sufficient: encourage them to clap hands, tap fingers, nod the head, shrug the shoulders, wriggle the hips, sometimes trying to *follow the leader*, who may be the teacher or a child from the class or group. If and when space allows, let them dance —both on the spot in contemporary twist-and-shake style and moving round the room.

Dancing with instruments should also be quite informal, the instruments being played in various ways —high and low, to the left and right of the body, in front and behind the body, drawing shapes, letters and figures in the air —working individually, in pairs, circles, short lines. For some children this is more stimulating than purely abstract modern dance.

Folk dancing can be accompanied by a rhythm group improvisation —at the same time providing active participation for those who cannot dance.

ii) Test the class with recorded examples of *instrumental music of contrasting styles*.

The two traditions —popular and conventional —should be mixed and merged, each used to further understanding of the other in listening and performance. The spontaneous spirit of pop music is attractive to most children and can be used as a link with other kinds of music: Latin-American, jazz, dance movements from suites and symphonies (e.g. waltz, polka), folk music of various countries. Each demands a different kind of concentration for the players to reflect in their rhythm-improvisation the characteristic tempo and rhythmic detail. Once established, test this by fading out the music, leaving the improvisers to continue playing; then reintroduce the music and see if they are still 'with it'. At first, fade out for only a couple of bars, but then increase the fade-out period each time.

iii) A variant on this idea is to finally *fade out the music altogether* and use the extant improvisation as accompaniment to a song or instrumental piece in similar tempo and style.

iv) For practice in playing at *different volume levels*, get the players to reflect the adjustments on the record-player as the volume control is changed from *pp* to *ff*, sometimes suddenly, sometimes gradually.

v) *Each instrumental group is given a number*: 1) drums 2) gongs 3) jingles 4) shakers 5) clappers 6) scrapers. Everybody improvises when the direction *tutti* (*all*) is given, but when a number is called, only that group continues. The idea can later be applied to individual players instead of groups, and this is a fine exercise for encouraging confidence and independence.

By taking an active part in the music, the listening powers of the participants are enlivened in a way which many of them would find almost impossible to achieve were they just sitting, although, of course, there are moments when sitting is good, desirable and even necessary.

Formal accompaniment using the vocabulary of basic rhythms

Having established the idea of improvisation by using a mixture of slow, quick and very quick sounds, a further vocabulary must next be built up, which can be drawn upon for improvisation. This is parallel to the situation in language where vocabulary is constantly being extended by participation in selected poems, stories, plays, games and miscellaneous activities. This further vocabulary consists of basic rhythms which may be practised to records as *follow-my-leader* games, and incorporated as formalised accompaniment to songs and poems, first by the teacher, then by some or all of the children singing and playing at the same time:

  i *pulse*

 ii *accent*

iii *weak pulses*

iv *time pattern*

 v *ostinato*

It is important to bear in mind that this formal practice is continued side by side with the improvisatory work outlined already, just as reading and writing in language lessons go hand in hand with oral composition and improvised drama.

i pulse

Pulse is the even regular throb which underlies all music; it is the life-giving heartbeat—in fact most often referred to as 'the beat'. The toe-tapping, head-nodding and hand-wagging that go on amongst people of all ages when they listen to particular types of music all clearly indicate physical response to a well-defined, regular pulse.

1   **Michael row the boat ashore**

The pulses in each bar can be produced by a repetition of any one sound, or by a mixture of different sounds:

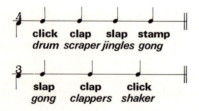

Pulse-playing is the very simplest form of percussion playing; as with free improvisation (see page 22) children need plenty of practice in accompanying songs of various tempi—slow, moderate and fast; also songs requiring various levels of volume— achieved by individual control or by varying the number or groups of instruments.

Continually encourage them to give an ear to the balance of voices and instruments, remembering that the instruments are *accompanying* the voices.

For additional practice in pulse playing use folk dance recordings, and to ingrain the feeling for pulsation get the children to move fingers, hands, arms, feet to the throb of the music (cf. page 23). Also use antiphonal groupwork, each instrumental group playing only when the teacher indicates; much phrase-consciousness is absorbed at the same time.

The 8421 Game is good for counting and concentration.
Music: any folk dance in 4 time which uses 8 phrases of 8 beats.
Divide the class into four groups. Each group plays in turn:

8 beats

4 beats

2 beats

1 beat

1 beat

The 8 phrases work out as follows:

Each group	Total effect
8 beats	4 phrases of 8 beats
4 beats	2 phrases of 8 beats
2 beats	1 phrase of 8 beats
1 beat $\Big\}$ 1 beat	1 phrase of 8 beats
	$\underline{\underline{8}}$

This may first be conducted by the teacher, then by individual children, but later played from memory.

A variant on the idea is for the players to improvise freely while they count the beats rhythmically as above.

Especially with young children it is possible to link this pulse work with fundamental movements. Every song suggests running, walking, skipping, swaying, so following the singing of a song, children can step and play these, thus providing a direct link with the teaching of note values:

♩ walk,   ♫ run,   ♩ ♪ or ♪♩ skip,   ½ slow walk.

Short stories can be invented by teacher and children to introduce these various fundamental movements; as a development of this a project of movements can be devised: e.g. toyshop, circus, Autumn.

ii accent

The pulses themselves are in turn grouped by regularly recurring stronger pulses known as accents, the ones in between being comparatively weaker, giving:

iii weak pulses

The children need experience in playing music of different metres: 2, 3, 4, 5 and 7 time:

3   Lightly row

Past three o'clock

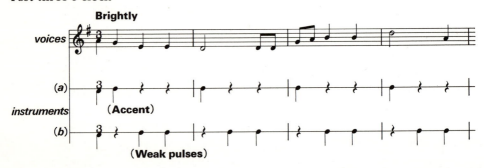

Always perform some physical movement during the silent beats, such as thumbing, flapping or sniffing. Sometimes, combine the two activities, one half playing a) and the other half b); at others, get each player to play accented and weak beats for himself.

With this experience it is an easy step to acquiring knowledge of bars, barlines and metrical time-beating. Once the ideas are established, give practice in placing the accent on beats *other* than the first beat in the bar; this is an introduction to syncopation.

iv time pattern

This is the actual rhythmic pattern of the melody. In a large majority of folksongs and simple songs the time pattern follows the word pattern (one note of melody for each syllable of lyrics), so the business of playing time pattern amounts to following the syllables of the words as they are sung. Some players find it easier to play the time pattern than the pulse. Time patterns may also be used as speech and rhythm exercises independent of the vocal line.

At first, insist that the words are spoken as they are played, since this controls tempo and establishes clear thinking. Later, the audible words can be dispensed with, the players thinking the words without speaking them aloud. As an alternative to song lyrics, poems, everyday phrases and proverbs may be used.

Time patterns may be used in various ways:

a) The words and phrases of time pattern may be split between the various body sounds:

4 Polly Wolly Doodle

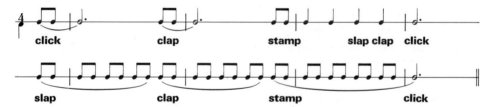

b) Antiphon

Antiphonal: a term used loosely to describe music that is performed first by one group and then 'answered' by another group (as, for instance, in the singing of alternate verses of the Psalms by the two sides of the church choir: *decani* and *cantoris*).

The time pattern is split between the players, each phrase being performed by a different group, suggested by the children, e.g.

Ten in the bed   phrase 1: drums

phrase 2: jingles

phrase 3: clappers

phrase 4: shakers

c) Canon

Canon: (means, literally, 'rule') strict imitation of a melody by one or more other parts at a given distance and at a specified interval.

The time pattern is played by several groups, each beginning at an agreed moment after the previous group. The result is most effective if each group uses a different body sound, possibly leavened by the addition of instruments:

group 1   clap and clappers

group 2   slap and jingles

group 3   stamp and drum

d) Counterpoint

Counterpoint: the simultaneous combination of two or more melodies which are of equal importance (e.g. a well-wrought descant provides counterpoint for the melody).

The time patterns of two or more songs may be combined, provided that they are identical in tempo and total number of beats; time-signatures and phrase-lengths may vary if desired.

e) Rondo

Rondo: a form in which the main theme occurs at least three times, separated by two episodes—i.e. contrasting sections. If the main idea is A, then the rondo is constructed like this: ABA^2CA^3

The time pattern of a song is used as the main theme of a ternary piece, ABA, or rondo, ABACA, in between which come the episodes—sections of rhythmic contrast, e.g.

1 time pattern of **Polly Wolly Doodle** chorus used as main theme of rondo

5   **CHORUS**

While the verses are being sung, the children improvise; later, these episodes can be performed by groups or individuals.

2 time pattern of **Polly Wolly Doodle** verse used as main theme of rondo

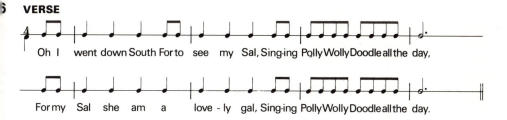

VERSE

Oh I went down South For to see my Sal, Sing-ing Polly Wolly Doodle all the day,

For my Sal she am a love - ly gal, Sing-ing Polly Wolly Doodle all the day.

During the singing of the chorus, rhythms are improvised by *tutti*, groups or individuals.

3 work either of the above without singing, but *thinking* the words and phrase lengths as they are played.

It is a comparatively easy matter for each child to sing and *at the same time* maintain for himself the pulse, accent or time pattern of what he is singing. It is a matter of coordination and constant practice. Some children find that movement helps their sense of pulsation; if they walk as they play they keep better time. Pulse, accent and time pattern may be mixed in various combinations, then it may be necessary to delegate the singing to one group and the rhythm accompaniment to individuals or groups. To help the performers playing pulse and accent, give them appropriate words to say as they play, or use French time names, e.g. *If all the world were paper.*

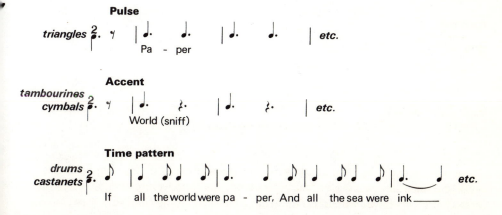

Pulse

triangles Pa - per

Accent

tambourines cymbals World (sniff)

Time pattern

drums castanets If all the world were pa - per, And all the sea were ink ____ *etc.*

Another way of combining the various elements of rhythm is to accompany the parts of a round:

3 parts   1st pulse
                         2nd time pattern
                         3rd accent

v rhythm ostinato

The next stage is to work on rhythm ostinato—a small piece of time pattern, i.e. a word or group of words—which is established then repeated obstinately over and over again as rhythm accompaniment. At first, choose those which begin on the

accent and use only one (♩), two-(♫ ♩) and four-(♬♬) syllable words.

Later, add those with three syllables (♬ ♩ and ♩ ♫ ♩).

   Two-, three- and four-word ostinati may be invented spontaneously to accompany records or songs, e.g. any of the following one-bar (three-word) ostinati could be used *pianissimo* to accompany *Golden slumbers*, whispered as words and/or played on rhythm instruments:

8

tea,   cof-fee, tea   A-lec, A-lec, John

Alternatively, they may be derived from the opening one, two or four bars of the song itself, repeating the ostinato as accompaniment to the whole song:

9   **One-bar:** This old man

This old man   **Play 8 times**

Two-bar: Weggis

We are off to the Weg-gis Late   **Play 4 times**

These may be learnt by rote, and linked with the reading of rhythm symbols; they become a musical *look and play* reading method. Then, preferably, prepare them on large charts which can remain on the wall, constantly in the children's view.

Children can memorise ostinati to

a) familiar words

b) French rhythm names

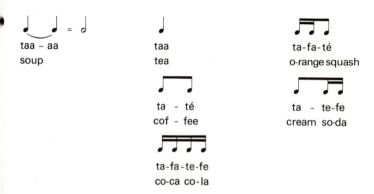

taa – aa   taa   ta-fa-té

soup   tea   o-range squash

ta - té   ta - te-fe

cof - fee   cream so-da

ta-fa-te-fe

co-ca co-la

Although some children grasp the latter, others seem to find them forever a mystery. On the other hand, many children who start working with natural speech rhythms accept the French rhythm names later as an abstract expression of everyday words. Moreover, children love words and therefore natural speech rhythms offer opportunity for tie-up between music and language, and are the strongest basis of all for the development of creative work.

Ostinati may also be practised in the Somervell shorthand:

4-bar ostinato

and used for games of *guess the title*.

Here is opportunity, too, for children to invent their own notation; indeed with secondary children this can well lead on to the study of notation used by George Self and David Bedford and a consideration of contemporary avant-garde composers.

Ostinato is the most difficult of accompaniment devices to maintain at the same time as singing. Three points arise:

a) the maintenance of the ostinati may be delegated to a special group (see Example 12, ostinati 4,5,6)

b) a one-word ostinato is not too difficult to perform at the same time as singing. Two or three groups can each perform a different word (see Example 12, ostinati 1,2,3)

These counter-ostinati are especially effective in the chorus of a song, each one-word ostinato being played by a different instrument or body sound.

12 Way down low

An effective four-part rhythm accompaniment can be built by using four basic rhythms, as follows:

4 parts   1st rhythm ostinato

2nd pulse

3rd time pattern

4th accent

The following are variants of the one-word ostinato accompaniment:

1 Each performer plays two words at the same time as singing:

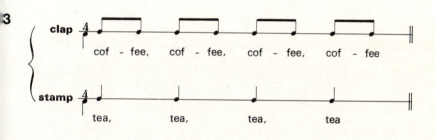

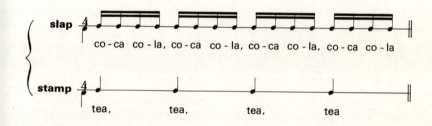

or three words:

2 The two halves of a song may be accompanied by a different one-word ostinato:

15 Polly Wolly Doodle

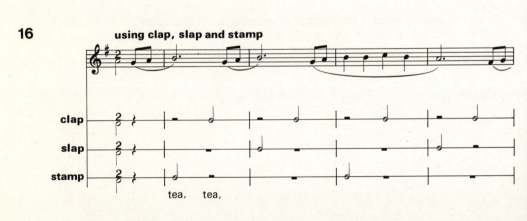

16

c) Some songs have a built-in ostinato and these are reasonably easy to perform while singing:

7 Steiner cuckoo (Chorus)

wren, cuc-koo, wren....

From this ostinato it is easy for the children to see the possibility of building an alternative ostinato by rearranging the words:

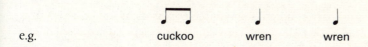

e.g.   cuckoo   wren   wren

Then the two may be used as counter-ostinato:

group I   sing melody and clap | ⊓ | (wren, cuckoo, wren)

group II   chant words of ostinato ⊓ | | (cuckoo, wren, wren)
                 and slap

Further ostinati can be built, still by using only the two words *wren* and *cuckoo*:

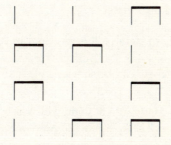

So it is possible to have up to six counter-ostinati; it depends on the inspiration, perspiration (and desperation) of the teacher how the work develops. Each repetition of an ostinato can be formed with a different body of sound; each word of the ostinato can be performed with a different body of sound; each individual can choose his own ostinato from those constructed. The results can be used to accompany other songs and records with the same tempo and style.

Arranging music for rhythm accompaniment

Much music is tremendously effective arranged for melody line plus rhythm accompaniment. It is of utmost importance to bear in mind the three factors mentioned in the Introduction:

1 the suitability of choice of effects and detailed content
2 the balance of melody and accompaniment
3 the general ensemble

Chorus songs are very useful for first attempts. Decide on the backing for the chorus and let this stand for each recurrence; the verses can be unaccompanied or have a minimal backing, possibly varied from verse to verse; then proceed to songs without a chorus.

Finally, especially with primary children, some suitable movement can be added in the form of dance or mime. In fact, short one-verse songs can be given length and interest by performing them three times:

  i vocal line only
 ii add rhythm accompaniment
iii further, add movement

thus contriving to build up more effect with each repetition.

Alternatively:
  i vocal line only
 ii add *some* rhythm accompaniment
iii add *complete* rhythm accompaniment

A short instrumental melody of eight or sixteen bars can be given similar treatment.

Another possibility, if the melody can be sung *and* played:
  i vocal melodic line only
 ii instrumental melodic line only (or combine with voices)
iii vocal and instrumental lines plus rhythm accompaniment

Whatever the existing material to be dressed up, the great thing is to use the effects skilfully and avoid using all instruments all the time. Bear in mind the way in which composers vary the texture by alternating and combining the different sections of the orchestra, keeping the impact of full orchestra for special moments. This is the composer's craft; teachers and children must learn to handle their materials with the same awareness of effect.

2 MELODY ACCOMPANIMENT

Introduction

Although most teachers are happy to handle work involving rhythm effects, many are anxious over the incorporation of melody accompaniment, since the latter requires a modicum of theoretical knowledge. If the teacher hasn't this, then he must have a mentor; the early work is not difficult to perform, so it is possible for the teacher to be taught by a colleague whatever he intends to teach his class. The work develops very gradually and many general practitioners find the pace well within their scope; the radio and television broadcast lessons are also a great asset to the non-specialist.

The first section of the book has dealt with means of accompanying with rhythm effects only. Gradually, melody effects may be added to make the accompaniments more interesting. The accompaniment not only enlivens the effect but becomes a vital part of the music.

The workout of techniques discussed in this section can be applied to examples drawn from publications of folk music and specially-composed modern works, or created by the children under the guidance of the teacher; especially useful then are the pentatonic melodies.

The pentatonic scale has five sounds and is virtually the major scale with the semi-tones omitted:

$$d \quad r \quad m \quad \left[f\right] \quad s \quad l \quad \left[t\right] \quad d'$$
$$1 \quad 2 \quad 3 \quad 4 \quad 5 \quad 6 \quad 7 \quad 1'$$

The scale can be based on any note and built up using the same pattern. Owing to the absence of semitones, any combination of melody and accompaniment is made available.

See also PART II, 1) **Further developments: Pentatonic techniques**, pages 82–3 and 2) **Children's original work**, pages 86–7.

Effects

Effects available

The effects available involve sounds of definite pitch; these are:
 i Voice
 ii Melody instruments

i **Mouth music, including whistling**

Again the voice is used virtually as an instrument, taking part in the melody or harmony of a piece.

ii **Melody instruments**

The classroom melody intruments include:
a) *pitch percussion*
b) *plucked and*
c) *blown instruments and*
d) *instruments capable of chording*
The tuning of all these is the standard A = 440. Check with a tuning-fork, and if any instrument is unsatisfactory, return the instrument to the manufacturer.

a) pitch percussion
bar instruments including: xylophone, glockenspiel, metallophone, chime bars; tubular bells; tuneable drums including tambours and timpani
improvised: glasses, bottles, flowerpots, metal bars and tubes

It must be emphasised that manufacturers do not always adhere to the technical terminology, but strictly speaking a *xylophone* has wooden bars (*xylon* is the Greek word for *wood*). The sound is short and dry, and in order to achieve an effect of length the sound must be repeated—by improvisation or as indicated in the score.

The *glockenspiel* has metal bars, usually of chrome-plated steel or aluminium. The sound is bell-like and has considerable sustaining quality; for this reason a number of the bigger instruments have a damping device which can be utilised as required; the smaller instruments don't need it—just as the short thin strings in a piano need no damper. Sometimes a glockenspiel player uses his hand as a damper to the vibrations.

The *metallophone* has matt metal or matt grey finish. The bars are made from a special metal alloy which gives a hybrid tone quality—dryer than the glockenspiel, yet with more sustaining quality that the xylophone.

Chime bars are also metal bars, but each is mounted separately on a resonating tube and can be used independently if required —as handbells are used—for melody or harmony. Some manufacturers make the bars of steel, others of metal alloy.

The bar instruments have *bars* of graded lengths mounted loosely on a frame, box or set of tubes which act as resonators. When struck by a beater, the bars vibrate, the longest bar to the player's left giving the lowest sound; all the bars are removeable, so that the player can work with only the ones he requires and also learn where the sounds 'live' in relation to each other.

The *beater* heads are of wood, plastic, rubber, leather or felt, some beaters being double-ended. Two are supplied with each bar instrument, but the children must be encouraged to experiment with other beaters, to find which gives the effect required at a particular moment. A hard stick produces loud sounds, a soft stick quiet sounds, but the volume can also be varied by the movement of the hand —swift or slow. This is comparable with the movement of a piano key which causes the hammer to hit the string abruptly or gently.

The bar instruments should be played with *two beaters*, one in each hand. At first, the children tend to play entirely with the writing hand, and need constant encouragement to use two beaters. This is necessary because the moment inevitably arrives when both hands are essential, so the non-writing hand must be practised from the start. The general principle is to alternate hands, so that the rhythmic continuity is maintained.

It is important to strike at the *middle of the bar*, playing with a very flexible wrist, allowing the stick to rebound from the bar, leaving it free to vibrate and give a clear sound. Each bar is clearly marked with its letter name but most manufacturers put the marking on the edge of each bar; since players naturally tend to strike where they see the letter-name marked, it is a good idea to relabel by sticking self-adhesive labels in the middle of each bar.

Miniature *tubular bells* are suspended from a frame, and are only commercially available in key G. They should be played with a wooden stick and hit at the point of suspension near the top of the tube.

Sizes and types of instruments

The bar instruments are available in various sizes: soprano, alto, tenor-alto, bass. Some instruments are *chromatic*—that is, two-tier, laid out like a piano keyboard with a complete set of 'black' and 'white' keys. Others are *diatonic*—that is, a single deck of 'white' keys with three or four spare parts which include F sharps, B flats and sometimes C sharps. These can be substituted as necessary for the white F s, B s and C s.

The makers of many pitch percussion instruments offer *carrying cases* (some convertible into table tops) and screw-in legs as additional items in their catalogues.

Probably the first purchase should be an instrument which doubles the children's singing voices; it is easier to pitch from this than from a smaller instrument, and it is, of course, far more useful for accompaniment. Later, the smaller (and larger) instruments will be necessary for part playing, but as a first investment one bar-instrument often has to be shared amongst the whole class.

For this reason it is probably best mounted in a position where everyone can see, and play by miming. Having learned an accompaniment in this way, then any child can come forward and play individually, if not in class, then in private practice time. Pitch percussion instruments are the most universally useful for instant music-making with all ages of beginners, especially in the nursery and infant departments where tiny fingers preclude the use of other types of instrument.

b) plucked instruments
table (or knee) harps: miniature concert harp, psaltery, chordal dulcimer, autoharp, guitar, banjo.
Improvised: one-string fiddle; tea-chest bass.
All harps have labels indicating the exact pitch of each string, so tuning is a comparatively easy business, once time has been set aside for the purpose.

For the enthusiastic craftsman, it is possible to make many instruments for a fraction of the price demanded by the commercial manufacturers. (See *Musical Instruments made to be played* by Ronald Roberts. Dryad £1.25.) It is important, however, that the craftsman should have a good ear, for bad tuning can lead to dire results.

c) blown instruments
recorder, harmonica, melodica (a blown keyboard instrument), accordion.
improvised or homemade: bamboo pipe, comb and paper, kazoo,
whistling, humming.

For years the *recorder* has been the universally accepted melody instrument for school use; in many cases the descant recorder is the first instrument to stimulate interest in instrumental playing. Some children progress to the larger sized instruments and are able to play in fine recorder and/or mixed ensembles. For others, the early experience on descant recorder is transferred to an orchestral instrument or the piano.

On the whole, the recorder would appear to have more attraction for girls than boys. Primary festivals are flooded with girl recorder players; the number of boys among them is small, and before they even reach the secondary school, the boys have 'slipped through the net.'

The *harmonica* is a little instrument too often neglected by teachers for classroom ensemble, mainly because it has humble associations with folk music and it is not a 'legitimate' instrument. But how much more attractive it seems to boys than the recorder; they like it for the very reasons that their teachers avoid it! It can be popped in the hip pocket and produced at informal moments, and in their opinion the tone quality is altogether, more masculine than the 'piping' recorder. Boys are often less conscientious than girls, so if the harmonica holds more attraction for them, it is surely logical to foster and involve that interest before it disappears. The harmonica is no more easy or difficult to learn than the recorder; it is just less familiar to the teachers. In a mixed ensemble of classroom instruments, the harmonica player can make as great a contribution as anyone else and learn as much of notation. Surely this consideration is more important than any of legitimacy. The interest thus fostered is reward enough; further, though, the experience may ultimately produce a fine harmonica player or more likely the enthusiasm and experience may later be transferred to an orchestral instrument.

Much the same can be said of the *melodica*; in addition it is an extremely versatile instrument, useful for:
1 infants whose tiny fingers cannot yet manage a recorder or harmonica
2 those who cannot manage the coordination required for recorder or harmonica; they find it comparatively easy to play consecutive notes with consecutive fingers
3 playing melodies or counter-melodies beyond the capacity of players on other blown instruments
4 those who do not enjoy the tone quality of recorders
5 players requiring a portable 'piano'
6 playing chordal accompaniment

Children can share an instrument by purchasing individual mouth pieces. Letter-names can be pencilled on to the keys if desired, for quick results in the classroom; this brings the melodica into line with the bar instruments which all bear letter-names.

d) instruments capable of chording
bar instruments, all the table harps, guitar, banjo, melodica, harmonica, accordion

All these can be used for single-line work, but can also play chords (sounds in combination).

Psaltery—a kind of harp with resonating box.

Autoharp—table harp with resonating box. Chords are played automatically without the tedium of fingering (as on a guitar), by depressing the bars with the left hand; the bars damp the strings not required. The right hand then strums the remaining undamped strings.

The *chordal dulcimer* is a rectangular resonating box over which are stretched four sets of three strings; each set is tuned to a chord, which may be plucked, or struck by a wide felt beater which straddles the three strings.

Choice of effects

For classroom ensemble work it is possible and desirable to involve all types of instruments—not only the simple classroom ones mentioned above, but also those which individual children are learning—orchestral strings, woodwind and brass, making a really mixed ensemble, embracing all levels of ability and achievement. Although a beginner string player may be shy about using his bow, he can always pluck (pizzicato) his instrument; a cellist, in particular, will help provide a much-needed bass foundation to an ensemble that is so often overloaded at the treble pitch end, especially if it lacks a guitar.

The school instrumental group can equally well be a mixed ensemble and should take its place as often as possible at assembly and school functions; this encourages not only the players, but also the would-be players not so far involved.

It is possible to achieve a great variety of tonal effects from a group of this kind, even though it may well contain players who achieve another kind of satisfaction altogether in their specialist ensemble groups—recorders, harmonicas, strings, woodwind, brass, etc.

Another worthwhile experiment is to try mixing two or three groups:

recorders and rhythm

woodwind and pitch percussion

recorders, melodicas and strings

brass and rhythm

harmonicas and autoharps

Let the children suggest possible groupings, then test and comment on their success or failure as tonal effects.

Building up a basic collection of instruments

In making a collection of rhythm instruments, choose those which will give a good variety of sound, giving opportunity for both orchestral and Latin-American effects. For rhythm instruments, the following are listed in order of general usefulness:

  i tambourine, castanets

 ii triangle, cymbals, drum, maracas

iii resi-resi

Invest as and when possible in top quality instruments. Meanwhile, the children can make music by accompanying their singing with body sounds, mouth music and homemade instruments. Better effects are obtained in this way than by buying a load of cheap instruments which have poor tonal quality and are not childproof when put to the test of day-to-day classroom work.

For a basic collection of melody instruments, a cross-section of the four types is the answer, keeping in mind a selection which will give a reasonably wide range of pitch.

Probably the most useful instruments for arousing interest in melody accompaniments are the chime bars. If resources are limited, a few may be bought at a time. People have different ideas about which few to buy first; possibilities are:

i C—F, then G—C, giving the complete scale of C major; later add F sharp, B flat, C sharp for the scales of G, F and D major.

ii Pentatonic scale of C: C D E G A:

iii C, F and G, giving tonic, sub-dominant and dominant in key C and tonic and dominant in key F.
Later add D, B flat, E and A, giving:
tonic, subdominant and dominant in G
tonic, subdominant and dominant in F
tonic, subdominant and dominant in D
and pentatonic C D E G A.

Next, or even first, a chromatic glockenspiel which will fill in the gaps left by unpurchased chime bars.

Range:

If and when funds allow, add a xylophone which, with its wooden bars, gives a hollow, dry sound providing contrast with the tone of the glockenspiel; for a basic collection the tenor-alto model with interchangeable B flats and F sharps is probably the most useful.

Range: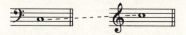

An autoharp gives good body to an accompaniment by providing chords and binding together the melodic strands. If possible, it is worth buying the twelve-bar model because of the large number of chords available.

Many teachers find that the melodicas are useful not only for their tone quality, which blends with other melody instruments, but also as an introduction to the layout of the piano keyboard. This knowledge is necessary for the bar instruments as well as the piano accordion. The alto size melodica gives a good pitch range for accompanying songs:

Before purchasing any instruments it is advisable to peruse dealer's catalogues with complete lists of instruments and prices; also seek the advice of the local music adviser who may be able to advise on financial as well as artistic aspects.

Accompaniments

Instruments may be used according to their suitability for a particular song. For the singers it is excellent ear training, since they must focus their ears differently to each instrumental colour supporting the voices. For the teacher, there is the big advantage of being able to face the class instead of sitting sideways on at the keyboard. The piano is often overpowering for the children's voices, and because of its size it isolates the teacher from the class to some extent. Music-making is a social activity and contact is far more easily achieved with portable instruments, when teacher and class can share enjoyment as they share in a story.

Often, particularly in accompanying traditional material, the piano is not needed; this leaves the teacher free to move amongst the class, organising and guiding them towards self-accompaniment. Especially for the teacher who is not a confident pianist, this piano-less work can be a great asset.

It is most important that before adding any accompaniment the children should know the melody line thoroughly. This was pointed out at the beginning of the section on **Rhythm accompaniments**, and it is, if anything, even more important when melody accompaniments are to be added.

Frequently the teacher selects a song or instrumental piece specially for the possibilities it offers for melody accompaniment; then it is preferable to teach the melody line beforehand. The business of coordinating melody and accompaniment is sufficiently engrossing and time-consuming in itself, without having to digress to keep the melody going.

There are exceptions to every rule, however, and occasionally it is fun to learn the accompaniment first.

Detailed content

Improvisation

Assuming some experience in improvising rhythms, it is an easy step for the children to improvise, on a bar-instrument, an accompaniment to a pentatonic melody, because all the sounds will blend well. The bar-instrument must be prepared with only the bars of the appropriate pentatonic scale, then the player can 'doodle' rhythmically with two beaters, using a mixture of slow, quick and very quick sounds, aiming to reflect and complement the rhythm of the tune itself. Other instruments can follow suit. (Compare PART I, 1) **Rhythm accompaniment: Improvisation**, pages 22—3).

Side by side with the improvisatory work must be taught the basic formal techniques of accompanying with melody instruments. As in the case of rhythm, the basic techniques of melody accompaniment are at first demonstrated by the teacher, who then hands over to the children. But as the work develops, it is important to help the children, at the earliest stage possible, to discover for themselves what sounds right in each situation.

This is obviously desirable as a form of ear training alone, and is therefore far more valuable than any of the teacher's directed activity.

But further, the exercise in listening, assessing and selecting is the very essence of melodic and harmonic improvisation; the principles thus established are absorbed and memorised subconsciously and later used spontaneously in improvisation in their appropriate context.

Formalised accompaniment using the vocabulary of basic techniques

Three factors must be considered when working out accompaniments with melody effects:

  i Bass support, independent of the melodic line
 ii Doubling of the melodic line in part or whole
iii Part playing—combination and development of i) and ii)

1 Bass support

a) drone bass
a single note acts as a kind of bagpipe drone note, continuously repeated.

1 All melodies based on the pentatonic scale may be successfully accompanied by any note of the scale used as a drone note.

2 Many based on diatonic major and minor scales and other modes may be accompanied by using the repeated keynote (doh) or the repeated fifth (soh)—whichever gives the best effect.

19 Girls and boys

There was an old woman

The rhythmic detail of the drone(s) is based upon any of the ideas in PART I, 1)
Rhythm accompaniment, pages 22—35:

20 The keeper

The melody takes two notes to one syllable of words so <u>both</u> must be played

If successful as a drone bass note, the doh and soh (tonic and dominant) will often work equally well at any pitch as an accompaniment. The tonic drone (or pedal note) will work with melodies harmonised entirely by I (tonic) and IV (subdominant) and the dominant drone with those harmonised by I (tonic) and V (dominant).

The drone may always be doubled at the octave (as above) while some accompaniments sound very effective with the keynote and fifth played together:

21 Carol: Heydum, heydum

An effective device for adding a very simple bass part on many occasions, the drone bass is at the same time a very useful means of launching the children on to melody instruments, since it involves a transference of familiar facts (basic rhythms) to a new situation.

Also, if the classroom is divided into two groups and the drone-note(s) sung, this in itself is an excellent introduction to part-singing. Many spirituals are based on the pentatonic scale and are therefore ideal for 11 to 18 year-olds as material for arrangements.

Once the idea has been established, let the children experiment for themselves and discover suitable drones for the songs they know or compose.

One string of a violin, viola, cello, guitar or banjo can be tuned to the required note(s) and used pizzicato or arco as a drone; small timpani can be used for the same purpose.

b) melody ostinato
a melodic fragment of two, three or four notes which is established, then repeated obstinately over and over again as accompaniment

1 All *pentatonic* melodies can be successfully accompanied in this way; the ostinati may use *any* notes of the pentatonic scale, but an effective ostinato can easily be made by taking a fragment of the melodic line:

22 Jim-a-long Josie

Hey Jim-a-long,— Jim-a-long Jo-sie, Hey Jim-a-long,— Jim-a-long Gee.

2-note ostinato accompaniments

long—————— Jim - a - long Jo - sie Jim-a-long Gee.

3-note ostinato accompaniments

Hey Jim-a - long—— Jim-a-long Jo - sie

ostinato accompaniments for Swing low, sweet chariot

2 notes   **3 notes**

Swing low,   cha - ri - ot — Com-in' for to car-ry me

2 Some *diatonic* melodies may be accompanied by the ostinato device; these have to be discovered by experiment, as opposed to the random selection that works for pentatonic melodies. Also, examples can be found in books of published arrangements for voices and instruments (see Appendix for book lists). Here is a three-note example:

23 Bye baby bunting

Again, the ostinati may be sung or played.

Rounds
In the performance of a round, every line is repeated part by part, acting, in effect, as a melody ostinato to the complete melody. Any one line can therefore be performed repeatedly by a soloist or group:

24   Morning is come

Start with short-lined rounds, and having sung the melody in the correct key, let the children discover for themselves on their instruments which notes match the words of each line. Having learnt a fragment by rote, it is good to make some written record as a memory aid, so let the children invent their own method of doing it, e.g.:

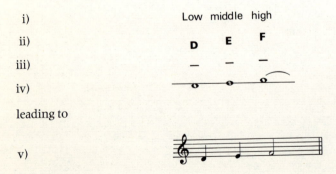

i)

ii)

iii)

iv)

leading to

v)

For more about notation see PART II, page 97.

c) two, three or four notes played as the *bass line of a simple chord sequence*. Melodies based on any scale or mode can be accompanied in this way; a number use two notes only —doh and soh:

25 Trot trot

But an even greater number come into the category of 'three-note' bass, using the first, fourth and fifth degrees of the scale —doh, fah and soh:

26 Early one morning

Pentatonic melodies may be harmonised with diatonic harmony or treated contrapuntally (see page 85).

A simple bass line can often be built from the left hand part of a piano accompaniment, especially where one left hand note accompanies a whole bar of the melody line.

Song books, published with guitar symbols, are a very useful source of inspiration for vocal-instrumental music-making.

27 Polly Wolly Doodle

The capital letters indicate the chord to be played by the chordal instruments; but more important, they are the notes which give the bass line of the chord sequence and can be played by any instrument —or even sung.

A capital letter indicates a major chord; a small 'm' (e.g. Em) at the side indicates minor; a small 7 (e.g. C7) indicates the dominant seventh (see *Part-playing c) chord groups*, page 56). The simplest way of writing a chord sequence is that of the jazz musician:

G G G D
D D D G

Blackboard summaries must be as eye-catching as possible so that the visual memory is instant; the above example is much harder to memorise written as:

G G G D D D D G

unless it is punctuated like this:

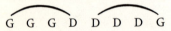

G G G D D D D G

Even then, the two-line layout is preferable. Memorisation is particularly essential for players of bar instruments, for it is extremely difficult to play from a score, even when it is on a stand immediately in front of the player.

Having established the bass line of a simple chord sequence, this may be used as a framework for further detail (see *Part-playing c) chord groups*, page 56).

ii 'Doubling' of melodic line

This involves 'doubling' of the melodic line in part or whole.

a) single note as introduction, interlude or postlude.

As a beginning to class activity, a child can play the initial note of a song, and, performed rhythmically, this can serve as an introduction:

28 Golden slumbers

Alternatively, the final note of the song may be used to make an interlude between verses, or a postlude:

29 Ride a cock horse

This is a very simple device, but quite sufficient challenge for some children. A development of the idea is for the performer to improvise rhythmically on the one note for a pre-determined number of beats.

b) tune snap
the children participate by performing short extracts from the melody, using the opening or closing few notes, or a refrain:

Heydum, heydum

 **at the end of lines 2 and 4**

Ten in the bed

Roll   o - ver!   Roll   o - ver!

These can be

1 discovered by the children themselves from a number of notes pre-selected by the teacher

2 learnt by rote

and/or

3 used in conjunction with pitch symbols.

They may be played by one child on any type of instrument or several children taking a note each on a bar-instrument or chime bars—handbell style.

At first, the teacher (and the rest of the class) may need to remind the performers by indicating with the hand the moment at which to play, but very quickly the players become independent. As in the case of rhythm notation, it is up to the teacher to decide if and when this work should be linked with pitch symbols; it can be another musical example of *look and play*.

Much pitch consciousness can be developed if the children move their hands up and down an imaginary ladder, showing the rise and fall of melody. Similarly, the melody may be shown graphically by a broken or continuous line:

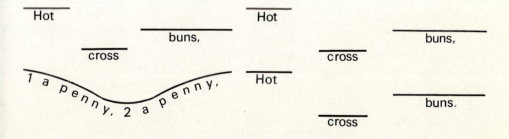

The tune snap may then be sung to tonic solfa (singing names), and then shown on the stave with both singing and playing names:

melody echo game
This may be played by the teacher and individual children or by two children. Using the sounds of the tune snap, player 1 plays them in a different order, making a new melody; player 2 echoes. If necessary the new melody must be repeated until the echo really materialises. The players then change over (cf. *rhythm echo game*, p. 67).

c) complete melody
In the same way, let the children discover and play complete melodies with a limited number of notes, the bar instruments being set out with pre-selected bars. Pentatonic tunes are obviously excellent material because of their limited number of sounds; recorder tutors, too, inasmuch as they start with two- and three-note melodies, then gradually extend to include more and more notes, and provide a suitable repertoire for playing on all types of instruments as well as the recorder. Moreover, the melodies are largely well known songs, so the class can sing, then play them.

As with tune snaps, the complete melody may be played by one or several children. If performed handbell-style, always use this as an a accompaniment to a continuous vocal line since this inspires confidence and rhythmic continuity. Remember too that a skeletal version of the melody is preferable if it will ensure rhythmic continuity; accompaniments cannot afford to 'slow down at the bends'.

Whenever possible have available a copy of the complete melody. Children can follow and pick out these melodies for themselves in music corner, the real readers hearing immediately if they mis-read, because the tune is familiar; it is all excellent ear- and eye-training.

Within every class the mixed ability problem may be solved by some members doing rote-playing and some reading parts on a selection of rhythm and melody instruments. This enables every player to contribute in a way satisfying to himself, so that although some individual parts may be extremely simple, the total result is effective for all participants. With carefully selected material the resulting sound is colourful and attractive, supplying a common ground between school and out-of-school music.

iii **Part-playing**—combination and development of previous ideas. Part-playing involves the children in taking responsibility for one of several different things being performed at the same time.

It may be a combination of ideas discussed in the previous sections:

two-part accompaniment

a) drone and ostinato

b) doubling of melodic line (whole or partial) with drone, ostinati or bass line

three-part accompaniment

a) doubling of melodic line with drone and ostinato

b) doubling of melodic line with drone and bass line

Or it may be a development of ideas discussed in the previous sections:

a) drone plus counter-melody

Once the idea of a drone bass has been established and throughly grasped, an alto, tenor or descant part may be added, making a third melodic strand. In the case of pentatonic melodies in particular these can be invented by teacher or children; alternatively, there are many examples in **Thirty Folk Settings for Children**, arr. Mendoza and Rimmer (Curwen).

The song can be finally dressed up by the addition of rhythm accompaniment so that there are six strands of activity:

e.g.			
	1	claves	pulse
	2	gong	accent
	3	maracas	rhythm ostinato
	4	drone	
	5	counter-melody	
	6	melody	

The children choose the instruments suitable for strands 4, 5 and 6, and decide on the rhythmic content of strands 1, 2, 3 and 4; then arrange the song by deciding the order of entry and also the ending of the song. The accompaniment can finish with the song itself or be continued as a postlude, the instruments finishing all together or dropping out one by one, possibly as a reversal of the introduction.

This is excellent preparation for handling material in their own original compositions

b) counter-ostinati

two or more ostinati are combined to make an accompaniment of counter-ostinati

1 pentatonic tunes: any notes of the pentatonic scale may be drawn on, but the counter-ostinati may well be a combination of fragments from the melodic line

2 diatonic tunes: once the initial ostinato has been established the counter-ostinati must be discovered by experiment or learned from the published arrangement

rounds

With reference to Example 24 on page 50, the entire melody can be accompanied by any combination of a) b) c) d), making counter-ostinato. Some will want to play the complete melody with the singers; finally, rhythm instruments can be added, too.

The arrangement can be built up by the class in a number of ways:

e.g.

introduction
1   ostinato a)
2   add ostinato d)
3   add ostinato c)
4   add ostinato b)
5   add rhythm instruments improvising
6   add voices (and instruments) singing complete melody twice
        1st time   *f*
        2nd time   *p*

coda
7   instruments continue
8   a final *sforzando*, repeating the last note

c) chord groups

Having established a bass line derived from a chord sequence, it can be used as the framework for further detail. The two-chord accompaniment (C and G) to **Bavarian song** (*The World Sings*, A. C. Black) can be performed in the seven ways shown in the example opposite

Bass line, consisting of only the roots of the chords:

a) on the accent at the beginning of each bar

b) on every beat

c) on every beat, but marking the accents with the left hand (stems down are for left hand (LH), stems up for right hand (RH))

Building two-note chords:

d) play 3 entirely with LH while RH plays the note next-door-but-one above (i.e. a third higher)—for major chords, 4 semitones above the root, for minor chords (marked 'm') 3 semitones above the root

Building three-note chords:

e) add to 4) another note next-door-but-one above, 7 semitones above the root, giving a complete triad. LH still plays the bass line; RH plays the other two notes with the two crossed beaters

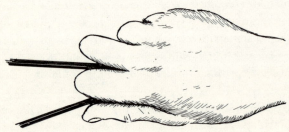

31 Bavarian song

f) same as 5 but splitting LH and RH

g) rhythmic improvisation of triad accompaniment

All but the last may be performed by groups of players, and the chords may also be played by chordal instruments.

d) recorder music adapted
The pitch percussion instruments (and others) can often be used to play parts intended for recorders in arrangements for recorders-and-strings and recorders-and-voices; and much recorder ensemble music can be adapted for general instrumental playing.

Notation

It is often the keenest children who acquire their own instruments (be it recorder, melodica, harmonica or orchestral instrument) and against a background of classroom music making activity, their progress is immediate and rapid, because they have already incidentally experienced the elements of notation; the challenge of an individual instrument quickly ties up all previous experiences, and further new ideas quickly take root and develop.

Once more, diversity and flexibility of method is probably best. When recorders, harmonicas and melodicas are in the same class, sometimes divide them into their specialist groups, sometimes into ability groups and at other times have them altogether.

The geography of the piano keyboard

A useful way of introducing children to the piano keyboard is by holding up a melodica and/or putting a large diagram on the blackboard:

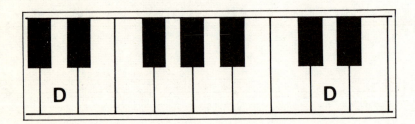

Point out that the black keys are arranged in a pattern of alternate groups of two and three. Think of the two as being a kennel; inside the kennel is a dog; the initial letter being D, this generally seems to be an effective way of fixing in the mind the name of this white key. Hence, it is logical to reckon that E, F, G lie above and C, B, A lie below it.

The next stage in learning the geography of the keyboard is to memorise the position of C at the foot of the two-groups of black keys, with E at the top; F at the foot of the three-groups of black keys with B at the top.

Play (and sing)-as-you-spell is a useful game:

DAD, BAG, CAD, AGE

CAGE, FACE

BAGGAGE, CABBAGE

for blown as well as bar-instruments.

In writing melody parts for children to play, there are three stages:

  i Capital-letter names beneath rhythm notation

 ii Staff-notation with letter names beneath

iii Staff-notation only

The bass part of **Steiner cuckoo** (Example 17) chorus would appear as:

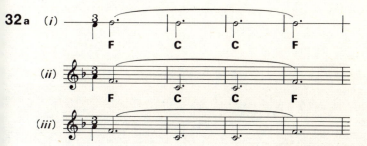

32 a *(i)*

       (ii)

      (iii)

n.b. parts should be written with a new line of music for each phrase of the melody

Alternatively, name the notes when they first occur, but not again:

32 b

or work in terms of a 'clue stave' before the clef:

33

Memorisation of 'lines and spaces' of the stave follows, and games can be devised for reading practice. The music corner offers marvellous scope for practising and preparing rhythm and melody accompaniments for class activity.

In all their work, take every opportunity of letting the children see what they are playing, singing or hearing. The *look and play* method is fundamental to all further skill in reading and writing. Writing is the complement of reading; it will naturally be behind the child's inventiveness, as in language; encouragement and guidance as and when needed are far more important than any rigid, formal scheme, especially at the start.

A useful and practical device is to turn a bar-instrument vertically, to show how alternate bars link with the lines and spaces of the stave —which may be the full five lines and six spaces, or a limited stave:

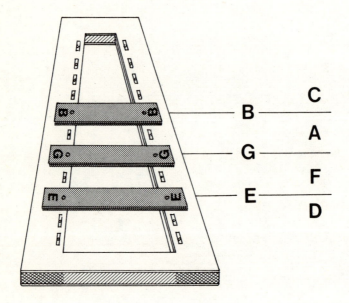

—and also use the hand as a five-line stave:

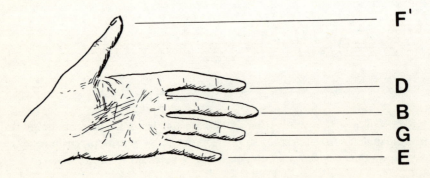

Arranging music for melody accompaniment

In the junior and secondary schools, children can gradually take on the playing of complete parts. Three factors must be considered:

 i Melody

 ii Bass and chords

iii Counter-melodies (alto, descant, tenor).

It is possible to combine these as follows:

34 Steiner cuckoo (Chorus)

Meanwhile, rhythm instruments accompany as follows, the rhythm ostinati being written on the blackboard:

35

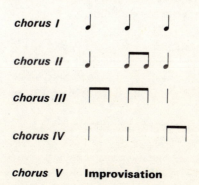

Practise these to appropriate words:

e.g.

wren   cuc - koo   wren

These could be performed with a different body sound for each verse, or a different group of instruments playing each time:

  i tambourines

 ii drums

iii triangles

iv castanets, claves

 v tutti

If the piano is used it must be played very economically to avoid drowning the delicate tone of the other instruments. It is often effective to play an upright piano with a sheet of newspaper slipped down between the strings and the dampers so that the hammers hit the strings through the paper, giving a crisp, dry tone not unlike a spinet. But the piano must be tuned to the same pitch as the instruments.

In building accompaniments, it is important to choose the most suitable instrument for each part. Here are some suggestions:

melody	descant recorder, glockenspiel, harmonica
alto and tenor parts	treble and tenor recorder alto melodica
chords	guitar, autoharp, accordion
bass line	large chime bars, tenor-alto xylophone, tenor-alto metallophone

A descant part must be played in the pitch at which it would be sung. An alto or bass part must lie *below* the range of the vocal line.

Remember that bar instruments are designed so that all unnecessary bars may be removed, leaving only those which are needed, and two performers can often perform on one bar-instrument. Also, bear in mind that the xylophone produces sounds of only short duration and these therefore need rhythmic repetition to give an effect of length;

in the **Steiner cuckoo** (above) the xylophone part is | ⊓ | rather than ♩.

for this reason. When a large metal bar-instrument is used for the bass line, its sustaining quality is considerable, and one sound lasts easily for one bar.

Dressing-up songs for beginners

  i thoroughly learn the song, then add one or more of the following accompaniments:

 ii rhythm (dramatic sound effects or otherwise)

iii melody line in part or whole (involving recorders, harmonicas, etc.)

iv bass, chords, counter-melodies

  v lengthen one-verse songs into three repetitions (or use verse 1 only to save learning many words of a longer song)

      e.g. a) voices only

          b) add rhythm instruments

          c) add melody instruments, too

 vi add movement

vii work out introduction, postlude and interlude

Arranging music for more advanced ensembles

Melody instruments

  i melody in part or whole

 ii bass

      a) derive bass line from chord symbols

      b) build out complete harmony

iii counter-melody: descant, alto, tenor parts;
alternate and mix these

Choice of instruments: choose suitable instruments for these
and include humming, whistling, comb-and-paper and kazoo

Rhythm instruments

  i pulse

 ii accent

iii weak pulses

iv time pattern   } using body sounds, mouth music and rhythm instruments

  v ostinato

vi improvisation

Choice of rhythm instruments depends on

      a) the type of song

      b) possible dramatic sound effects

      c) the melody instruments playing at a particular moment

Alternate instruments and vary the rhythms they play

      a) in long songs from verse to verse

      b) in short songs during the repetitions

Build introduction, postlude, interlude.

PART II

Further developments and application of these ideas to children's original work

1 FURTHER DEVELOPMENTS

Rhythm

More uses of ostinati

i) The ostinati derived from the opening of one song may be used to accompany
another song with similar time signature, tempo, phrasing and style:

36 Alive, alive O

ii) Counter-ostinati
The opening 8 pulses of several songs may be used as counter-ostinati, each instrumental group playing its own ostinati as accompaniment to an entire song with 8-pulse
phrases:

37 Joshua fit de battle of Jericho

Alternatively, use 6-pulse ostinati for a song with 6- or 12-pulse phrases.

iii) Fix an ostinato for one group to play and give the rest the opportunity of

a) creating their own ostinati (see page 30)

b) improvising freely

iv) Try 'throwing an ostinato' from group to group. A group may be of miscellaneous
instruments or all of similar ilk, e.g. drum group, shaker group.

Games with speech rhythms

Lists of words can be built under all kinds of headings:

names of people, cars, aeroplanes, football clubs, pop groups, flowers, vegetables, breakfast cereals, fruits, railway stations

A recently learned song can be followed by building a set of words relating to its topic:

pirates

1 syllable	2 syllables	3 syllables	4 syllables
wind	pirate	gold moidores	skull and crossbones
sail	treasure	treasure chest	Long John Silver
gun	cutlass	marlinspike	powder monkey
blood	galleon	Spanish Main	pieces-of-eight

These word lists may be used for a number of games:

i echo game with words
Having established a pulse, the teacher calls a word or group of words, which is immediately repeated by the children as a call-and-echo game.
   The next stage is to do the same but to add body sounds for every syllable spoken. The call may also be made by individual children. The challenge of the game is to 'keep the pot boiling' with no hesitation or pause between the call and the echo; that is, the pulse must not be broken; it is better to make a mistake in the detail than to stop the continuity.

ii echo game without words
The teacher plays a pattern only once without speaking any words and immediately the class echoes it. The game should be played by using all four body sounds in various ways, e.g. ♩ ♫ ♩ can be performed entirely by any one of the body sounds, or it may be varied:

iii rondo echo game
Use call-and-echo for the various episodes of a 'rondo' song, the words springing from
the topic of the song.

These games are useful for all stages and ages of children as ear-training exercises. They
are particularly useful with the youngest children, and may be developed into little
pieces:

At Christmas time

Each class listed Christmas words of one, two, three and four syllables:
e.g.

1	2	3	4
star	reindeer	mistletoe	Father Christmas
toys	holly	Christmas cake	decorations
wine	ivy	Bethlehem	Christmas pudding
snow	Jesus	Christmas tree	carol singers
	pudding		

With the youngest children the list was spontaneously compiled by means of pictures.

The reception class put together some words to make a phrase; showing their disbelief in Father
Christmas, they invented:

A

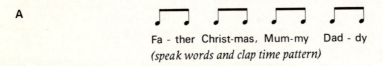

Fa - ther Christ-mas, Mum-my   Dad - dy
(speak words and clap time pattern)

*This was used as a rondo theme (**A**). The two episodes (**B**) consisted of name-calling by*
individual children, then by the whole class, of Christmas presents they desired

B   watch, bridesmaid doll, typewriter, gun, sweetshop, rifle

This complete piece was then built:

AA   **B**   **AA**   **B**   **AA**   *coda: sh . . . .*
choral   *solo*
speech   *voices*

Second year infant.
Again the words selected were used as a rondo main theme:

A

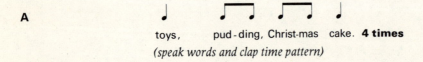

toys,   pud - ding, Christ-mas   cake. **4 times**
(speak words and clap time pattern)

B *(episode) call and echo the names of Christmas presents:*

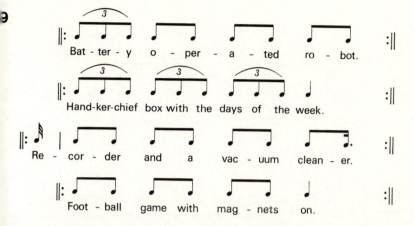

This was later extended to a full rondo with a second episode:

C *(new words) and a further repeat of the main theme:*

A	B	A	C	A	*coda*
	episode		*episode*		
	1		*2*		

The coda (tail-piece) was shouted:
And a Christmas tree!

Word-calling games

Lists of words can be used to develop rhythmic independence by 'calling' them
to music; recorded music is best since teacher and class are then free to concentrate
on the speech rhythms which can later be used as song-accompaniments.

i) The teacher sets going the recorded music and establishes the pulse which is taken
up by the children moving their hands to the pulse beat.

ii) The teacher points to the words, moving up and down (and across) the list(s) whilst
the children speak the words rhythmically to the music.

iii) The children add knee slaps for every syllable spoken.

iv) The children follow the teacher's hand and perform without speaking the words,
the knee slapping alone making an accompaniment to the music

This, together with everything discussed so far, can be done perfectly well without
reference to notation, but the opportunity of coordinating speaking, hearing and
playing with reading is one hardly to be missed:

40 beverages

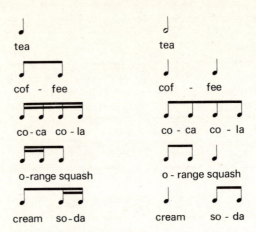

Presented in triple time the same words appear as:

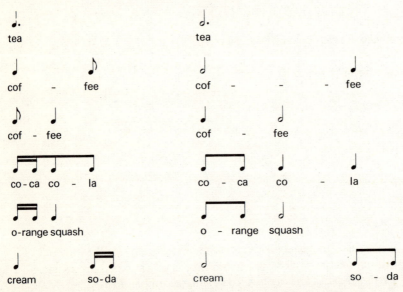

and may also be presented in compound time and with anacrusis.

The word-calling games can be played by pointing to:

a) words only

b) words and notation

c) notation only

Ostinati games

i) Word-calling of this kind is useful activity in its own right; it can also be developed by grouping words into one-, two-, three- and four-word ostinati. At first the teacher points these, but later the children can point, and the whole class participate in the building of ostinati. Having used them as accompaniment to recorded music, they can later be used to accompany songs and build pieces.

Second year infant:
Having built their word lists of fireworks, the children paired the names of their favourites into two-word ostinati which were then used as introduction and accompaniment to a song previously learnt:

1   Cracker Jack

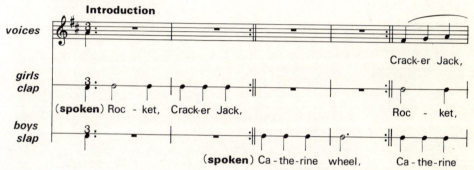

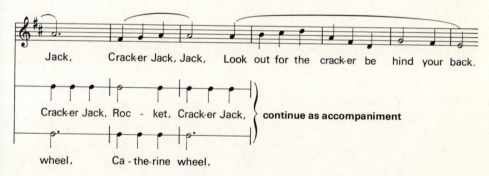

Incidentally, the signature tune for the news on BBC 1 television is a fine example of a four-beat ostinato:

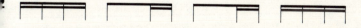

but is phrased to produce:

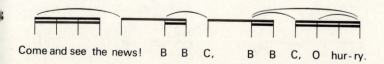

ii) Another method of pointing ostinati is to group the words in pairs, then, in pointing, the teacher's hand moves across the board:

44a

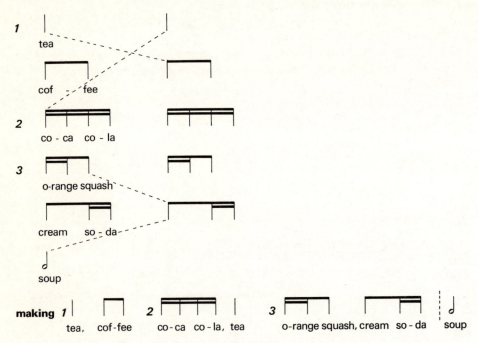

Or group them in threes as an accompaniment to music in triple time:

44b

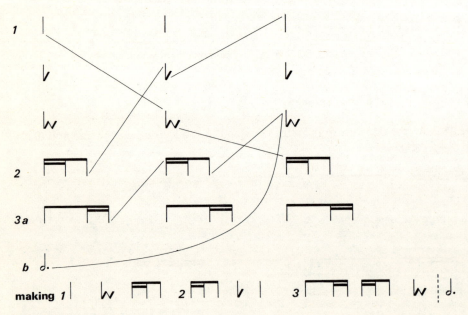

iii) Many dances are based on the ostinato principle, so these can be played to accompany recorded examples; some of the most well known are:

45

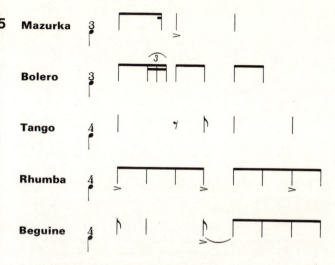

iv) A further possibility is to play pulse, accent, weak beats, ostinati, whilst following the rhythm symbols on the blackboard:

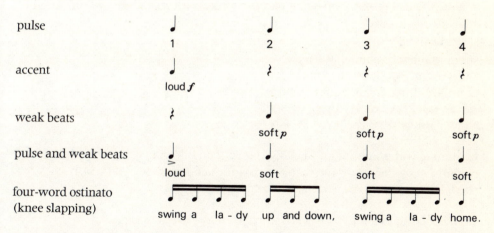

a) at first, every beat should be pointed, but as the practice develops, only the beginning of each line (bar) needs indicating. It is important that the pulse should be counted aloud,—the sounds spoken and the silences whispered.

b) each line may be repeated any number of times according to the direction of the teacher (and then individual children) or the four lines may be played consecutively.

c) while the recorded music plays, the children make any sound they like when they see a notehead, but they must be silent during the rests; there must be some physical movement during the rests—arm flapping, thumb 'upping' or sniffing.

Group work

The following assignments can be done with the three types of rhythm effects only, but melody effects may be incorporated too.

i Accompany an 'own choice' song with rhythm instruments (see Examples 46—47).

ii Compose a television jingle, using spontaneously improvised melody, plus rhythm ostinati (see Examples 48—51).

iii Writing lyrics
Seeing that much melody making is based upon speech rhythms, a complementary idea is to:
a) write new verses to songs
b) write lyrics for instrumental pieces (see Example 52).

iv Compose a story or narration incorporating songs and poems with a common theme; then add dramatic sound effects and introduce recorded music to establish atmosphere and finally bind together the various ideas.

v Write original poems, stories and plays and draw pictures to link with the idea of dramatic sound effects.
Suggested topics:
Spring, Summer, Autumn, Winter,
The Seasons, November the Fifth,
Christmas, Toyshops, Factories, A Farm,
The Seaside, The Sea, A Visit to the Fair,
Negro Spirituals

vi Starting with three or four carefully chosen sounds, decide what the sounds are reminiscent of, then use those characters and/or happenings to build a story, play, poem or picture —or even paint a picture or pattern.

vii Describe an event, using narration, sound effects and drawings.

viii Make up a radio play, i.e. in terms of sounds only; or a television play which links sounds with a series of appropriate illustrations used like a film projector.

ix Build a collage of sounds: abstract, human, animal, machine

Another facet of the work is to include tape recorded sounds. Much interesting and fascinating experiment can be done by playing back recorded sounds at double and half speed and various volume levels, in reverse or on loops e.g. record the sound of a nail scraped across the ridged side of a rubber hot water bottle; played back at half speed this makes a marvellous sound of a geiger counter. Such experiments in sound are also useful in connection with the avant-garde music-making of innovators.

i 'Own choice' song with improvised rhythm accompaniment
Group work.
The boy's choice was mostly popular material in the form of pop songs or television jingles with narrative interspersed. The girls were more conservative, choosing songs they had learnt in school. One of the infant groups, lost for melody recall at the crucial moment of recording, improvised the opening of the melody

46a Duke of York

After this, the original melody was sung. In the improvised accompaniments extensive use was made of the time pattern, especially in the infant groups:

46b Humpty dumpty

46c Old Doc Jones

In some cases the time pattern was coupled with the pulse, and occasionally the accent. A few groups used counter-rhythms and a considerable number added introductions and postludes. A fourth year junior group also made effective use of tacet (is silent) *during the verse, except for an underlining of the colour name in the lyrics, introducing instruments only for the chorus sections:*

47 O won't you sit down?

The introduction consisted of eight pulses played tutti.

ii Television jingles

Group work.

The infants and lower juniors produced 'food' songs rather than advertisements. Some of the second year juniors and most of the third and fourth year captured the true idea of a selling gimmick.

All had in common the strong feeling of rhythm ostinato used as an introduction, then maintained as a backing to the jingle, which was sometimes spoken, sometimes sung; often the sung jingle started in the pentatonic scale, but adventured further afield afterwards.

As a result of this assignment, a number of individual songs materialised from the second year junior class:

48 Pork sausages

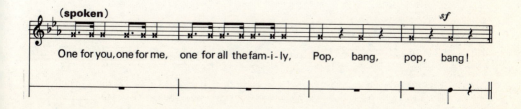

49 Eggs, liver and jelly

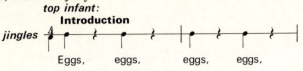

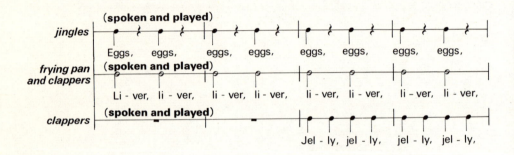

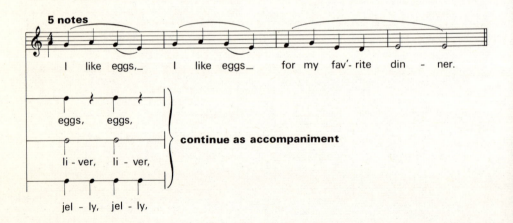

Meat and potatoes

first year junior:

Introduction

scraper

Meat, meat, meat, meat,
(**spoken and played**)

5 notes: D-A

Verse 1

I like meat, I like meat ev'-ry sin-gle day, I like meat,

(*scraper*)

meat, meat,....

I like meat ev'-ry sin-gle day,

(**spoken**)

Po-ta-toes, po-ta-toes, po-ta-toes, po-ta-toes, po-

4 notes: E-A

Verse 2

I like po-ta-toes, I like po-ta-toes ev'-ry sin-gle day,

-ta-toes, po-ta-toes,....

I like po-ta-toes, I like po-ta-toes ev'-ry sin-gle day.

continue as accompaniment

51 Coffee

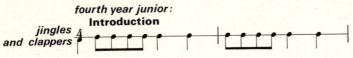

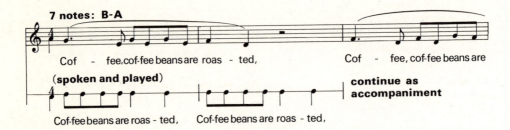

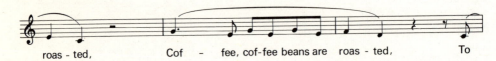

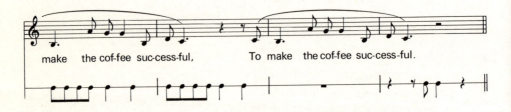

In performance the rhythm ostinato relapsed into

iii Words to existing melodies

Starting with Robert Salkeld's **March** *from* Second Concert Pieces for Recorder *(Schott),*
which uses only four notes—G A B C—the children wrote lyrics and the piece was extended
for a Christmas concert:

March	*a) recorders only*	*with piano*
	b) voices only	
episode	*a)* **Good King Wenceslas**	*melody played*
	b) **The Holly and the Ivy**	*by all who could*
		manage these

(cont.)

March   *Tutti: voices with all melody and rhythm*

                             instruments playing parts as suggested in PART I, page 63.

52   **Come to the party**
         fourth year junior:

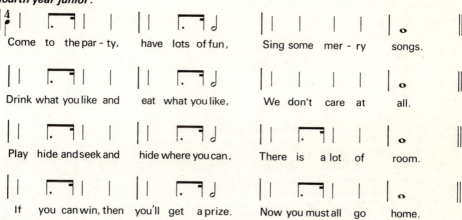

Come to the par - ty,   have lots of fun,   Sing some mer - ry   songs.

Drink what you like and   eat what you like,   We don't care at   all.

Play hide and seek and   hide where you can,   There is a lot of   room.

If you can win, then   you'll get a prize.   Now you must all go   home.

Melody

Discovering chord sequences

Just as children can discover melodies for themselves, so they can discover harmonies too, chord progressions being discovered from pre-selected chords; this is parallel to the use of pre-selected bars for melody playing.

For example, **Polly Wolly Doddle**: two three-note chords are played on chime bars:

D   A
B   F sharp
G   D

The class listens to the effect, sings the component notes of each chord, then decides which fits best with the opening note(s) of the melody. Having decided on the G, the chord of G is played tremolo (rapid repetition of a note or alternation of two notes) while the others sing the melody, and by listening to the match of melody and chord, indicate when it is necessary to change to the other chord, and when to return to G. The chord progression is finally established as:

G   G   G   D
D   D   D   G

The whole project can obviously be worked vocally as an exercise in part-singing. Later, the choice can be extended to three chords.

Vocal and/or instrumental improvisation

Improvisation on the chord sequence can follow. At first, move freely up and down the notes of the chord (or extended chord) in any rhythm which rides that of the melody (i.e. it doesn't match but complements it). Later, passing notes can be added, making stepwise melodies over the chord sequence. The basic rhythm can be varied to produce various dances (see Example 45).

This, of course, is virtually the art of the jazz musician who improvises variations over the memorised chord sequence of a tune, so that he is performing an instantaneous Chaconne; each repetition is called a chorus. In the classroom, as in jazz, each chorus may be taken by a different performer or group of performers. Since all are working over the same chord basis, collective improvisation should fit!

Chord sequences as a basis for composition

Improvising in this way may produce melodies worth capturing as song material. The following hymn resulted from a group of teenagers experimenting with bar-instruments and guitar:

53

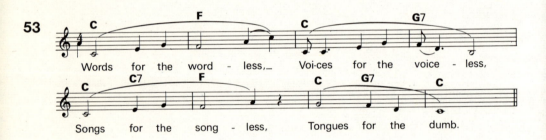

Words for the word - less,_ Voi-ces for the voice - less,

Songs for the song - less, Tongues for the dumb.

Pentatonic techniques

A pentatonic melody can be accompanied in a variety of ways. It may, of course, be harmonised by a diatonic chord sequence and it has also been shown how any pentatonic melody may be accompanied by a drone note or melody ostinato. The 'melodic fragment' type of ostinato having been grasped, the children can invent their own ostinati drawing on any notes of the pentatonic scale. Some examples are shown opposite.

Any one of these ostinati makes a suitable accompaniment to the melody line; equally well, any combination of two or more will be effective as counter-ostinati,

some performed vocally, some instrumentally; the children should decide. A fast-moving ostinato can be played as a descant on a high-pitched instrument, e.g. one of the *small* glockenspiels; it would be cumbersome played at a lower pitch by a larger instrument.

To make an extended item the various verses and choruses of a song may be accompanied by combining melody and rhythm instruments using the various ostinati shown above:

e.g. **Swing low**

chorus 1	ostinati 4,5,6
verse 1	unaccompanied girls' voices
chorus 2	ostinati 1,2,3
verse 2	unaccompanied boys' voices
chorus 3	ostinati 1–6

Rhythm instruments may then be added to finally dress up the arrangement (see
PART I, 1) **Rhythm accompaniment**)

all choruses	pulse	drum
	accent	gong
	time pattern	claves
	rhythm ostinati	scraper, shaker
all verses	claves and shakers play the time-	
	pattern of the refrain	

55

Finally, add introduction, interludes and postlude.

Further treatment of pentatonic melodies

Because of the particular construction of the pentatonic scale any melody based upon
it can be played and/or sung canonically, one part starting after another, in any
number of parts and at any number of beats behind each other:

56

or accompanied by augmentation (half speed) or diminution (double speed) of itself:

57

Two or more pentatonic melodies in the same key may be combined contrapuntally, provided that the number of beats is identical:

A summary of pentatonic techniques

 i Harmonise diatonically
a) with instruments
b) vocally in close harmony

 ii) Treat contrapuntally
a) parts sing the melody in canon, augmentation, diminution
b) accompaniment may be in the form of a drone (single or double) and/or ostinati drawn from the pentatonic scale (melody fragments or constructed independently).
c) combine with one or two other pentatonic melodies

The practice of these techniques offers enormous scope for invention as an activity in itself and also as introduction to more purely creative work.

2 CHILDREN'S ORIGINAL WORK

The greatest difficulty for the teacher ambitious to tackle creative work is first, how to start and secondly, how to organise the material as class and/or group activity. The element of fear naturally stands as a barrier, especially perhaps the fear of attempting ideas that may on surface glance appear to be too simple.

In PART I much consideration has been given to the development of rhythmic spontaneity. As a springboard for melody-making, we can use the children's natural feeling for rhythm coupled with their gradually developing experience and knowledge of basic rhythms. Once started, they tackle melody-making with enthusiasm, even though their ability varies enormously, of course.

Use of the pentatonic scale for melody-making

The pentatonic techniques may be applied to both vocal and instrumental melody making; it is virtually impossible to compose an ugly melody from the pentatonic scale. The scale itself can be built on any note, but this starting-note need not be the key centre of the melody:

built on C: $\overline{E_1 \quad G_1 \quad A_1}$ | $C \quad D \quad E \quad G \quad A$ | $\overline{C^1 \quad D^1 \quad E^1}$

built on G: $B_1 \quad D_1 \quad E_1 \quad G \quad A \quad B \quad D \quad E \quad G^1 \quad A^1 \quad B^1$

(The pentatonic scale starting on F sharp uses only the black keys of the piano keyboard.) Any note of the scale may be used as an accompanying drone-note (see PART I, **2) Melody accompaniment: Formal accompaniment using the vocabulary of basic techniques**: pages 45—48) but in key C the only double-drones available at the fifth are:

C and G   D and A   G and D   A and E

With its lack of semitones (and consequent lack of dissonances) the pentatonic scale offers great freedom to the beginner at improvisation and composition, since all the sounds blend well together, making any combination of melody and accompaniment pleasing to hear; the work can thus be the launching-pad for invention based on other scales and diatonic chord sequences. This idea is the inspiration of Carl Orff, whose teaching method begins with it.
   The degrees of the pentatonic scale may be introduced gradually and used to

double the speech rhythms of words, phrases or verses selected or written by the children. Any limited selection of these notes can be taken, although Orff starts with those of the pentatonic scale built on C : E and G, expanding to E G and A, D E G A, then C D E G A; later, notes of the extended scale are involved (see Examples 59—67).

Speech rhythms are therefore used as the basis of melodic phrases and accompaniments, rhythm and melody being blended and alternated with infinite variety and effect. Improvisation is the backbone of invention, and when the children have improvised something that they wish to record in writing, then the experience makes obvious for them the need for notation (see pages 44—49, 82, 83).

At first the choice of notes for melody and accompaniment is fairly random, but by constant experiment the children become more and more critical and selective about the most effective sounds. Selections of sounds other than the pentatonic may, of course, be made, and these will be discussed later. The hesitant beginners gain confidence with a limited selection of sounds, while the ambitious are quickly ready to enjoy the challenge of wider scope.

Vocal music

A very simple way of beginning melody making is to set a four-line verse to music, then add accompaniment, using the various techniques considered so far. As the melody-making proceeds from two notes to the extended pentatonic scale, a knowledge of form develops too, starting from the most simple form of four similar phrases:

A A A A moving to the variants of three similar phrases plus one contrasting phrase
A A A B, A A B A, A B A A and on to:
A B A B, A A B B, A B B A and later:
A B A C and A B A C A (rondo),
and A B C D
These forms can also be applied to instrumental work.

i Melody-making using two notes
Class work.
Aim: to develop rhythm and melody ostinati with words sprung from a topic
a) *speak the words*
b) *add body sounds*
c) *add rhythm instruments*
d) *add melody instruments*
These ostinati were built by the children and combined with choral speech or sung verse to make little compositions (shown on next page):

59 Summer holidays

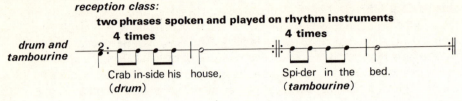

60 The zoo

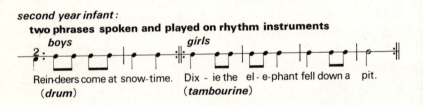

November the Fifth

Top infant class work

The words were used for name calling on two notes, then built into the piece shown opposite which the children decided should be introduced by a television jingle which they all knew:

61 Fireworks

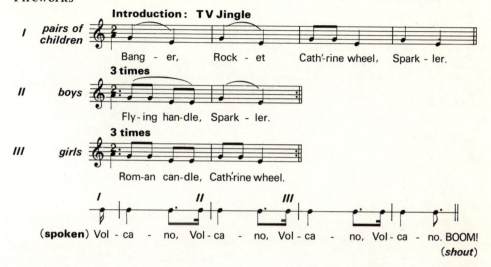

ii Melody-making using three notes
Class work

a) *lyrics—free choice*

b) *melody—any choice from five notes: C D E G A (the same melody for all four lines)*

c) *accompaniment: rhythm ostinati*

d) *drone bass: choice of C D E G A*

Experiments were made using this material in various orders of entry, sometimes beginning with the drone bass, sometimes with the rhythm ostinati performed a) antiphonally b) contrapuntally); with and without words:

62 Bubble says the kettle

Rhythm Ostinato accompaniments

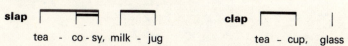

63 Ning, nang, nong
second year junior:

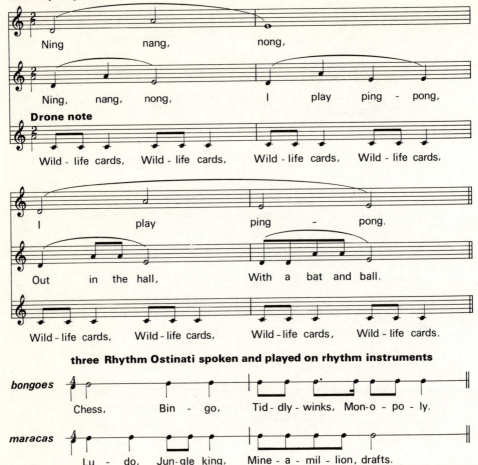

three Rhythm Ostinati spoken and played on rhythm instruments

iii Melody-making using five notes
Fourth year junior
Class work

Poem In the brook the Autumn leaves
Sail like little fairy boats;
On the gently gliding stream
See, each tiny vessel floats

Percy Young

64

After the poem, the two phrases were repeated four times, first antiphonally, then contrapuntally:

a) *words only*

b) *add rhythm instruments only*

c) *add melody instruments only,*
   improvising on five notes —   *reflecting the*
   xylophone and glockenspiel   *speech rhythms*

d) *combine words, rhythm and melody instruments*

e) *combine the two groups contrapuntally*

                                                           trill on   *sf*
bar-less instruments   *crescendo*   *BOOM!*

Teenage group work:

65   Freedom calypso

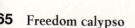

iv   Melody-making using extended pentatonic scale
Work on the pentatonic scale with particular reference to Negro spirituals produced
the following words and music:

From a sixteen year-old boy at a youth art centre

66 Ev'rybody who am living

1. Ev'ry - bo-dy   who am   liv-in',   Ev'-ry - bo-dy   got-ta   die.
2. Ev'ry sin-ner   who am   liv-in',   Ev'-ry sin-ner got-ta   die.

Rich'n   poor,   great and small,   Got-ta   meet   in judgement hall.
Young and old,   short and tall,   Got-ta   meet   in judgement hall.

From a teenage group at a youth conference

67 Freedom

Free - dom,   free - dom,   Free-dom from   the

chains that   bind   us,   From   all   hate   and   sel - fish   pride.
(Free - dom)

Free us O Lord,   Free us O Lord,   Free us from our chains O   Lord.

Instrumental music

When the building of instrumental pieces is pursued as a classroom activity, shortage of instruments is more of a problem than it is for the creation of instrumental accompaniments. But much can be worked in the form of rhythm-melody effects, by using two (often very uneven) groups, one improvising rhythm, the other melody, using the two groups, sometimes alternating, sometimes collaborating.

Even with only one bar-instrument in the class, two players can perform at the same time, and the improvisation in both groups can be collective or solo, or an alternation of these. Another possibility is to divide the melody group into drone, ostinato, and improvised solo. Of course voices may also be used as instruments, the children doing vocal improvisation to words, nonsense syllables or vocal sounds, e.g. 'la', 'oo', 'mm'.

A third group can do movement improvisation; this acts as a great stimulus to the instrumentalists; another variant is for some children to play rhythm instruments *as* they move.

i new tunes for old

Play the time pattern of an existing melody—rhythm group on rhythm instruments, melody group on selected bars, for example. A march can be 'invented' by playing the time pattern of **Grand Old Duke of York** or **The saints go marching in,** or a waltz by playing **Lavender's blue** or **Clementine**. The children decide on the plan, which might be:

The saints	3 choruses
	a) rhythm only
	b) melody only
	c) tutti

A more detailed plan:

chorus I	phrase 1 } phrase 2. }	tutti
	phrase 3	melody
	phrase 4	rhythm
chorus II	phrase 1	melody
	phrase 2	rhythm
	phrase 3 } phrase 4 }	tutti

A blackboard synopsis can be built up, but it is up to the teacher to steer the plan so that it doesn't become too detailed to memorise ultimately. It is always wise to keep a copy of the blackboard summary, otherwise much time can be wasted next time in recalling what was achieved in the previous session.

ii Take the characteristic rhythm of a step: run, walk (march) skip, sway; *or a dance:* waltz, tango, mazurka, etc. (see Example 45).

rhythm group   establish the rhythm ostinato. If a large melody instrument is available include that as a member of the rhythm group in the form of a drone or melody ostinato. If desired, the characteristic rhythm can be 'caught' rhythmically from a record.

melody group   improvise around this, sometimes reflecting the rhythm ostinato, sometimes purposely breaking away for the sake of variety.

Having established the content, then work out a plan as in i) above. After experience and confidence have been gained, the teacher should guide the children to adopt and put into practice the simple forms suggested for song-writing.

iii Rondo

Use the opening eight bars of a published piece as the main theme (A) of a rondo —
A B A C A form. Make the first episode (B) a purely rhythmic improvisation for an
agreed number of bars (during which everyone counts *1 2 3, 2 2 3, 3 2 3, 4 2 3*, etc.)
and the second episode (C) melodic, the players using notes from the pentatonic scale
in the same key as the main theme, over a drone or ostinato:

68 **A Chinese market**
students:
group improvisation using extended pentatonic scale

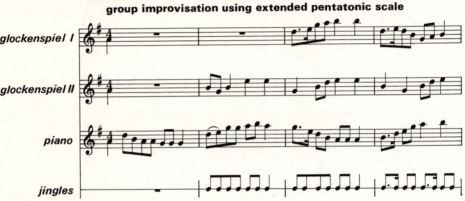

Use of sounds other than the pentatonic

Vocal and instrumental music can likewise be improvised and composed with a free
choice of scale or mode (limited or extended selection of sounds): major, minor or
chromatic scales; any of the modes (i.e. white keys only).

Second year junior girls group work
The song was introduced and accompanied by improvisation on two glockenspiels:

69 **Fireworks all the day**
second year junior girl:
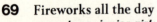

Fire-works all the day,   In the night the beau-ti-ful   spark-lers are in time,

Love-ly spark-les   all   the way,   With the spark-les ev'-ry-where

You will know they're there.   Bangs here,   bangs there, You will know they're there.

Alternatively, the selection of sounds may link with those used in a recently learnt song or instrumental piece.

Vocal music

Much can be done in the way of spontaneous improvisation without any instruments; it all depends on the enthusiasm and encouragement of the teacher. Children quickly catch on to the idea of inventing new words to known songs; from this they can evolve the alteration of certain melodic phrases to suit the meaning of words. This is especially applicable to verse-repeating songs, where the melody remains the same, regardless of the word-sense; it is then an easy step to song composition.

Informal conversations, questions-and-answers and stories can be sung (instead of spoken) freely or with a limited number of notes, and even developed into opera.

This is, on the whole, most easily achieved with young children in the informal atmosphere of the familiar classroom setup, when children are unselfconscious and quickly responsive. On the other hand, improvised opera and folk-opera are very much in the province of secondary school, given the happy coincidence of teacher and children who enjoy dramatic activity.

Instrumental music

Free choice of scale or mode

i The player improvises on rhythms and notes of his own choosing, which may be anything from one note to the complete chromatic scale (see Examples 70 and 71).

ii The descriptive element becomes the stimulus for improvised music to a play or story, e.g. describing a character: a king, giant or fairy; setting a mood: space, ghosts, jungle, water.

iii As a development of ii), work out a story in music with dramatic sound effects, mood music, themes and songs for the characters. This can be an existing story, one specially invented for the purpose, or an experience that the children have shared.

iv Another aspect of the work is to experiment with a wider vocabulary of sounds and effects in aleatoric fashion, following the ideas of George Self as summarised in **New Sounds in Class** (Universal Edition). Such experiments, exciting and adventurous in themselves, are also an immediate link with the current trends of twentieth century composition techniques, and help the children to familiarise themselves with the sounds of avant-garde music.

Free improvisation

Group work
Although the children were sitting in groups, the idea of free invention resulted, in many cases, in individuals improvising without any group feeling. There were a few exceptions to this, where there was good inter-reaction and rhythmic unity. In most groups the children had a

mixture of melody and rhythm instruments, and some incorporated voices too. There was a good deal of apparent wastage, but intense involvement just the same:

70 March

71 Syncopation dance

Notation

The bar-instruments are heavensent for young composers.

  i They select the sounds they are going to use, and remove superfluous bars from the instrument.

  ii Having worked out their melody, they can indicate the outline beneath the words, because the letternames are on the bars—a very easy transference of sound into sight:

72

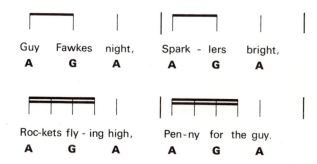

iii With guidance, the melody can then be transferred to staff notation, and accompaniment added too.

Class and group work

During creative work the constant aims must be those of activity and discovery, developing an awareness of the raw materials of music. The satisfaction is not so much that of producing marvellous compositions (any more than in language) but of pleasure in handling the raw materials and creating together something entirely original, as distinct from re-creating a score; the two activities go hand in hand, each furthering the understanding and enjoyment of the other.

  In projects of this kind, the discovery, criticism, selection and rejection of ideas and final collation of material involve the participants in intent listening, which is then transferred to their own performances of re-created music and appreciation of music for listening; then they must surely understand far more vividly how composers communicate with their listeners in terms of tempo, rhythm, melody, tonal colours, dynamics and so on.

  It is important to give regular opportunity for group work during:

  i Music workshop, when the class divides during the music session itself (this depends on premises and equipment).

ii General group activity, when music is one of many activities. One group devoted to music-making can isolate itself without disturbing or being disturbed

iii Break time, when one group only is allowed to work.

Thus, opportunity is provided for following up class ventures and for free experiment, which often provides the fertilising ground for further creative work. The children may be grouped in various ways: similar or mixed ability, girls, boys, or mixed.

The following work shows further examples of projects in school and club, applying in a very simple way some of the ideas suggested in this book. It is described and transcribed as fully as possible in an attempt to help teachers who have not yet tried this kind of work themselves.

At Christmas Time

Second year junior

Class work

The class divided into four groups and each chose words to use as rhythm ostinato:

73

Three groups decided to add a melody instrument carrying only E G A, the resulting melody ostinato being:

74

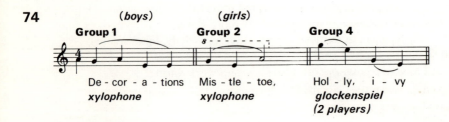

2 Children's original work

The next task was to make a melody for an existing Christmas rhyme, again using only E G A; the melody was to be the same for every line. The children thought of all the various permutations:

E G A, A G E, A E G, G A E, G E A

It was decided to use G E A. the fact that it had already been adopted by group 2 didn't worry them. The 'composition' was then discussed and summarised on the blackboard:

Introduction	1 decorations (4 times) played and sung	2 mistletoe (4 times) played and spoken	3 wine (4 times) spoken	4 holly-ivy (4 times) played and spoken

Interlude   bar-instruments introduce song melody   G E A

glockenspiel alone (twice)

glockenspiel and xylophone (twice)

Song

Christmas is coming, the geese are
    getting fat
Please put a penny in the old man's
    hat.
                 } Glockenspiel only, G E A

If you haven't got a penny, a ha'p'ny
    will do;
If you haven't got a ha'p'ny, God
    bless you.
                 } Add xylophones I, II ostinati

Coda   Shout   Happy Christmas!   Hurray!

The full score appears on the next page as:

The Red Shoes

Class work

This was a project involving every class in the school. We listened to the Saga record of **The Red Shoes**, *the second side of which is mostly a series of dances which were shared between the classes as topics for composition: Waving, Tapping, Stamping, Swaying, Mischief, Running, Prayer, March.*

a) the rhythm

each class listened to its chosen music and improvised to it until a common rhythm ostinato emerged; suitable verses were then written to fit

b) the form of the verse was A A A B, i.e. three lines repeated with the last line different. The melody to be selected from the notes D E G A.

c) the accompaniment

1) the class, having constructed the melody, then sang with time pattern accompaniment on rhythm instruments and the vocal melodic line doubled on a bar-instrument

2) later, further rhythmic accompaniment was added, and a double drone bass; the children selected from C G, G D, D A, A E.

d) finally, introductions and postludes were added

At the end of the term the work of all classes was collated into a final presentation. The story was written in their own words by a group of children and read by a narrator. The reading was interspersed by class performances of their own songs, while another group was responsible for mime and dance throughout (see examples on pages 102, 103).

Marching songs

Speech rhythms. Each of the five classes spoke the marching song the children had made up; then they were spoken contrapuntally, the time pattern of each being reflected by a different instrumental timbre (see Example 78).

76

Mischief song

O sil - ly you, you've lost your shoe, And
O cock - a - doo you've found your shoe, O

so have you, you naugh-ty girl.
luck - y you, the cow went moo.

Stamping song

fourth year junior:

78 **8 bars** *knee slapping* **once through**

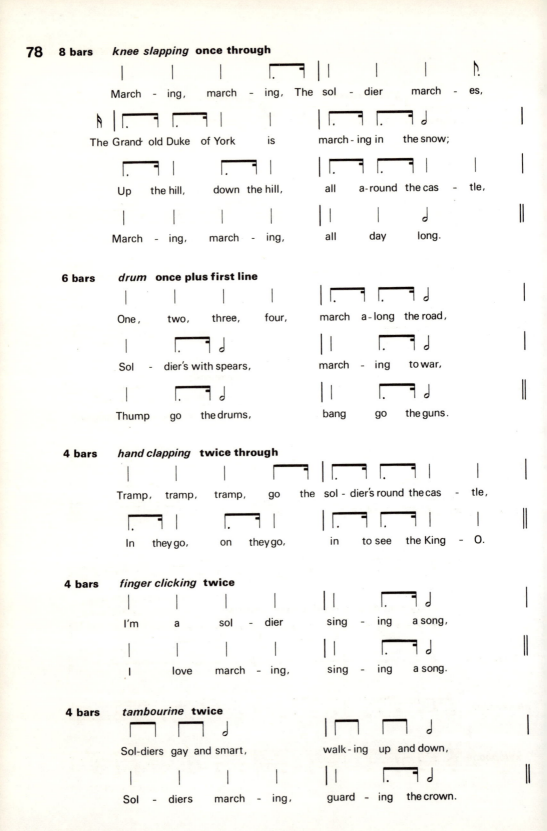

March - ing, march - ing, The sol - dier march - es,

The Grand old Duke of York is march - ing in the snow;

Up the hill, down the hill, all a-round the cas - tle,

March - ing, march - ing, all day long.

6 bars *drum* **once plus first line**

One, two, three, four, march a-long the road,

Sol - dier's with spears, march - ing to war,

Thump go the drums, bang go the guns.

4 bars *hand clapping* **twice through**

Tramp, tramp, tramp, go the sol - dier's round the cas - tle,

In they go, on they go, in to see the King - O.

4 bars *finger clicking* **twice**

I'm a sol - dier sing - ing a song,

I love march - ing, sing - ing a song.

4 bars *tambourine* **twice**

Sol-diers gay and smart, walk - ing up and down,

Sol - diers march - ing, guard - ing the crown.

November the Fifth

Group work
Lyrics, melody, backing and sound effects were composed by the children and woven together
into imaginative compositions; third year work was developed further in language lesson where
delightful poems materialised. Names of modern fireworks lend themselves well to creative music
making!

a) lyrics   inspired by the word lists
b) melody   composed on two or three notes selected from the pentatonic scale
c) ostinato accompaniments
  1) body sounds
  2) rhythm instruments
  3) melody instruments
d) drone note   own choice
e) introduction   firework noises

Some groups spoke the rhyme they had made up, but some invented quite sophisticated melodies
extending over the range of a tenth. One delightful spontaneous melody came from a little
blonde girl in the second year whom I could not hear until the recording was played back:

'9   Guy Fawkes night

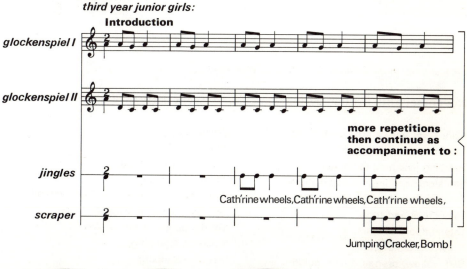

Fourth year junior boys

Group work

As an introduction, the melody was played, then repeated as accompaniment to the song. Occasional drum exposions happened in the background and a rhythm ostinato was spoken and played:

80

See the rockets flying high
fourth year junior:

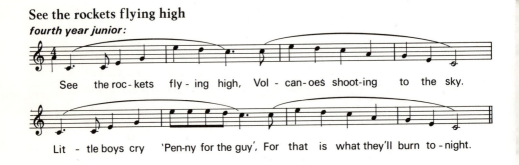

These are two of the poems written by third year juniors:

November Fifth (written by a girl)

Fairy silver with a little silver light
Golden rain, raining gold.
Jumping jack jumping about.
Sparklers sparkling here and there.
Rockets zooming by;
They break and form
Lots and lots of stars.
Fireworks blue, green,
Red, yellow, orange, silver, golden.
On goes the fire; the swirling flames twirl.
The guy will soon be dead.
The sky is smoky, the grass is dewed.

Firework party (written by a boy)

Glittering sky,
Blazing fire,
Guy Fawkes burning,
Children playing,
Rockets shooting and bangers exploding.
Jumping jacks moving like frogs.
All the people wearing gloves,
Children stamping,
People stamping,
That's what firework night is like.

APPENDIX

APPENDIX I

Example	Source	
1 Michael row the boat ashore		*Trad.*
3 Lightly row		*Trad.*
Past three o'clock		*Trad.*
4 Polly Wolly Doodle		*Trad.*
7 If all the world were paper		*Trad.*
8 Golden slumbers		*Trad.*
9 This old man		*Trad.*
Weggis	Something to Sing, Book 1	*OUP*
12 Way low down	More songs of the New World	*Holmes McDougall*
17 Steiner cuckoo		*Trad.*
19 Girls and boys		*Trad.*
There was an old woman		*Trad.*
20 The keeper	Separate sheet	*Novello*
21 Heydum, heydum		*Trad.*
22 Jimalong Josie	Oxford School Music Books, Beginners' Book 1	*OUP*
Swing low, sweet chariot		*Trad.*
23 Bye baby bunting;	Rhymes with Chimes	*OUP*
24 Morning is come	Graduated Book of Rounds	*Novello*
25 Trot, trot		*Trad.*
26 Early one morning		*Trad.*
29 Ride a cock horse		*Trad.*
31 Bavarian song		*Trad.*
36 Cockles and mussels		*Trad.*
Clementine		*Trad.*
37 Joshua fit de battle of Jericho		*Trad.*
41 Cracker Jack		
46 Humpty Dumpty		*Trad.*
Old Doc Jones	Eight American Dances	*Paxton/Novello*
Duke of York		*Trad.*
47 O won't you sit down?		*Trad.*

APPENDIX 2

There is an ever-increasing supply on the market of arranged traditional material and specially composed modern works using voices and instruments. Some publishers run a series:

Belwin Mills	Junior Ensemble Series
Boosey and Hawkes	Percussion Series
Chappell	Group Music Making Series
Chester	Junior Music Series
Keith Prowse EMI	Design for Music Series
Novello	Group Music Making Series
OUP	Percussion Series
OUP	Oxford Instrumental Series
OUP	Music for Ensemble
Universal	Voices and Percussion Series

Other Publishers:

Faber

Feldman/EMI

Galliard/Stainer and Bell

Hohner

Holmes McDougall

Lengnick

Schott

Weinberger

SOME USEFUL TEXT BOOKS

Infant

Shepherd	My Kind of Playgroup Music	*PPA Publication*
Pope	Growing Up with Music	*OUP*

Infant Junior

Hall	Music for Children	*Schott*
Chatterley	Sticks and Stones	*Novello*

General

Winters	Musical Instruments in the Classroom	*Longman*
Dobbs	The Slow Learner and Music	*OUP*
Paynter	Sound and Silence	*CUP*
Schafer	The Composer in the Classroom	*Universal*
Self	New Sounds in Class	*Universal*
Dankworth	Jazz: An Introduction to its Musical Basis	*OUP*

Instrument Making

Dankworth/Priestley	Make Music Fun	*Dryad*
Roberts	Musical Instruments Made be Played	*Dryad*

MAGAZINES FOR THOSE CONCERNED WITH MUSIC IN SCHOOLS

Music in Education	Macmillan Journals Ltd, Brunel Road, Basingstoke, Hants. RG21 2XS
Music Teacher	Evans Brothers Ltd, Montague House, Russell Square, London WC1B 5BX
Set to Music	107/111 Fleet Street, London EC4

RECORDS FOR CHILDREN: See page 126

GROUP MUSIC MAKING BOOKS

McLullich	Music Alive	*Oliver and Boyd*
Addison	Children Make Music (Teacher's book and 3 pupils' books)	*Holmes/McDougall*
Schools Council Project	Time for Music 1) Infant 2) Junior	*Arnold*
Lawrence/Montgomery	Words and Music (Teacher's book and 4 pupils' books)	*Longman*
Bulman	Music in Action (3 pupils' books)	*Hart-Davis Educational*
Walker	Sound Projects	*OUP*
Currie	Music Workshop	*Holmes McDougall*

JUNIOR CLASS BOOKS

Winters	Music Together Series	*Longman*
Maxwell-Timmins	Music is Fun Series	*Schofield and Sims*
Dobbs/Fiske/Lane	Ears and Eyes Series	*OUP*

SECONDARY CLASS BOOKS

McMurtary	Group Music Making	*Longman*

TRADITIONAL SONGS FOR ADDED ACCOMPANIMENT

Infant

arr Buck	Oxford Nursery Book	*OUP*
arr Dobbs/Fiske	Oxford School Music Books, Beginners' Series	*OUP*
arr Fletcher/Denison	The High Road of Song	*Warne*
arr Matterson	This Little Puffin	*Penguin*
	Sixty Songs for Little Children	*OUP*
arr Seiber	Hungarian Nursery Rhyme Book	*Schott*

Infant Junior

arr Carter	Discovering Music IV: Making Music	*Ginn*
arr Harrop	Apusskidu	*Black*
arr Offer	Children's Songs from Other Lands	*Paxton/Novello*
arr Seeger	American Folk Songs for Children	*Doubleday*
arr Wilson	Music Time	*OUP*
arr Wiseman/Northcote	Clarendon Books of Singing Games, I and II	*OUP*

Junior

arr Adams-Jeremiah	The Autoharp	*Lengnick*
arr Green	Chorus	*Puffin*
	Chansons de Notre Chalet	*Universal*
	The Railways in Song	*Chappell*
	Sing a Tune	*Universal*
	Diamond Jubilee Song Book	*GG Association*
	The Song Tree	*Faber/Curwen*

Junior Secondary

arr Brace	Something to Sing, Books I and II	*CUP*
arr Brocklehurst	Pentatonic Song Books I and II	*Schott*
arr Hyman and Rice	Sing a Round Books I and II	*Galliard/Stainer and Bell*
arr Jenkins/Visocchi	Mix 'n' Match	*Universal*
arr MacMahon	Sundowners' Song Book	*OUP*
	Look Away	*Universal*

Secondary

arr Brace	Something to Sing, Books III and IV	*CUP*
ed Dankworth	Jug o'Punch	*OUP*
	Eleven Hymn Tunes	*Weinberger*
	Sing True	*Religious Education Press*
arr Noble	Three Chords and Beyond	*Novello*
arr Smith	Faith, Folk and Clarity	*Galliard [Stainer] and Bell*

Infant Junior Secondary

arr Horton	The American Songbook	*old*
arr MacMahon	Songs of the New World	*Holmes McDougall*
arr MacMahon	More Songs of the New World	*Holmes McDougall*
arr Veal	The Singing Cowboy	*Boosey and Hawkes*

MODERN SONGS FOR ADDED ACCOMPANIMENT

Infant

Barnard	New Nursery Jingles	*Faber/Curwen*
Elliott	Fingers and Thumbs	*Galliard/Stainer and Bell*
Gray	Knives, Forks and Spoons	*Lindsay Music*
Offenheim	If Snowflakes Fell in Flavours	*Universal*

Infant Junior

Holt	Merrily Dance and Sing	*Boosey and Hawkes*
Swift/Clauson	Sing a Merry Song	*OUP*
	Singing Fun	*Harrap*
Swift/Wheatley	Things to Sing	*Arnold*

Junior

Jenkyns	Little Spanish Town	*Novello* (*Sheet*)
Parry	Three Unlucky Men	*OUP* (*sheet*)
Perry	Old Mister Noah	*OUP* (*sheet*)

Junior Secondary

Balkin	We Live in the City	*Universal*
Chappell	The Daniel Jazz	*Novello*
Hurd	Rooster Rag	*Novello*
Jacob	Animal Magic	*OUP*
	Twentieth Century Hymn Tunes	*Weinberger*

Secondary

Bennett	The Aviary	*Universal*
Hurd	Jonahman Jazz	*Novello*
Jenkyns	Rumba	*Novello*
Rose/Cook	Folk and Vision Book of Words and Melody	*Hart-Davis Educational*
	Songs of Sydney Carter in the Present Tense, Books I, II, III	*Galliard/Stainer and Bell*

ARRANGEMENTS OF TRADITIONAL MATERIAL FOR VOICES AND INSTRUMENTS

Infant

arr Adair	Ding Dong Bell	*Novello*
arr Blackburn	Sixes and Sevens	*Feldman/EMI*
arr Gavall	Nursery Songs	*OUP*
arr Mendoza	Let's Sing and Play	*OUP*
arr Rees	Sing with Chimes 1	*OUP*

Infant Junior

arr Chatterley	Seventy Simple Songs with Ostinato	*Novello*
arr Maughan	Tommy Thumb	*OUP*
arr Mendoza/Rimmer	Thirty Folk Settings for Children	*Faber/Curwen*
arr Murray	Eight English Nursery Rhymes	*Schott*
arr Rees/Mendoza	Rhymes with Chimes	*OUP*

Junior

arr Binney	Haliky Daliky	*Belwin Mills*
arr Longstaff	Jimalong Josie	*OUP*
arr Mendoza	Ten London Songs	*Chappell*
arr Mendoza/Rimmer	Thirty More Folk Settings	*Faber/Curwen*
arr Rees	Sing with Chimes II	*OUP*

Junior Secondary

arr Bergman	The Drummer Boy	*Schott*
arr Hosier	Mango Walk	*OUP*
arr Kendell	Sir Geoffrey's Book	*Chester*
arr Pont	Music Workshop Books I, II	*OUP*

Secondary

arr Bergese	Europa im Lied (Great Britain)	*Moseler/Novello*
arr Green	Linstead Market	*OUP (sheet)*
arr Pitfield	Kalinka	*OUP (sheet)*
arr Tate	The Shepherd Boy's Song	*OUP (sheet)*

MODERN COMPOSITIONS FOR VOICES AND INSTRUMENTS

Infant

Adair	Ring a Ding	*Novello*
Barnard	Play for Singing	*Faber/Curwen*
	Musical Playlets Series	*Universal*
Kendell	Edward Honey Bruin Bear	*Chester*
Murray	Wee Willie Winkie	*Schott*
Rees	Tunes for the Music Makers	*Hohner*

Infant Junior

Bentley	Songs to Sing and Play	*Novello*
Burnett	Poltergoose	*Chester*
Orff/Keetman	Music for Children Book 1	*Schott*
Southam/arr Dankworth	Play Songs	*Feldman/EMI*

Junior

	Music Plays Series	*Chester*
Crosse	Ahmet the Woodseller	*OUP*
Odam	Angry Arrow	*Chester*
Orff	Music for Children Book II	*Schott*
Lord	Nonsongs	*Universal*
Rodney-Bennett	The Midnight Thief	*Belwin Mills*

Junior Secondary

Cole	Flax into Gold	*Chappell*
Lord	How the Stars Were Made	*Chester*
Orff/Keetman	Music for Children Books III, IV	*Schott*
Russell Smith	The Emperor and the Nightingale	*Boosey and Hawkes*
Stephenson	Singplay	*Hohner*
Winters	Sing It and Ring It	*Universal*

Secondary

Chappell	Mak the Sheep Stealer	*Universal*
Crosse	Meet My Folks!	*OUP*
Hurd	Diversions	*Novello*
Pope	The Song of the Ass	*OUP* (*sheet*)
Williams	The Moonrakers	*Weinberger*
Winters	Bite, Frost Bite	*Universal*

CHRISTMAS MUSIC

Arrangements of traditional Christmas music for voices and instruments
Infant Junior

Hofman	Christmas Songs with Chimes	*Paxton*
arr Rees/Mendoza	Carols with Chimes	*OUP*
arr Winters	A Christmas Story	*OUP*

Junior

arr Hunter	Carol of the Huron Indians	*Faber/Curwen (sheet)*
arr Rees/Mendoza	More Carols with Chimes	*OUP*

Junior Secondary

arr Edwards	Eight Christmas Carols from Europe	*Belwin/Mills*
arr Green	Little Bull	*OUP (sheet)*
arr Hunter	A Calypso Lullaby	*Faber/Curwen (sheet)*
arr Murray	Four Christmas Carols	*Schott*
arr Parry	Christmas Day and Every Day	*Chappell*
(with recorders)		
arr Bergman	Nine Christmas Carols	*Schott*
arr Dinn	In Bethlehem City	*Schott*
arr Warren	Suite of Carols with Recorders	*Novello*

Modern Christmas Compositions for Voices and Instruments
Infant Junior

MacNeil	In Bethlehem Town	*Keith Prowse/EMI*
MacNeil	Three Carols to Sing and Play	*Keith Prowse/EMI*

Junior

Kendall	The Shepherd's Tale	*Chester*
Williamson	Christmas Songs for the Young	*Weinberger*

Junior Secondary

Deutsch	The Christmas Story	*Universal*
Gilbert	One Holy Night	*Keith Prowse/EMI*
Hinton	At Christmas Be Merry	*OUP (Sheet)*
Hinton	Rejoice and Be Merry	*OUP (Sheet)*
Murphy	Timothy's Miracle	*Schott*
Orff/Keetman	The Christmas Story	*Schott*

Secondary

Cartwright	Christmas Jazz	*Boosey and Hawkes*
Jenkyns	Gloria	*Keith Prowse/EMI*

INSTRUMENTAL ENSEMBLE

TRADITIONAL
Infants

arr Adair	A Little Anthology of Folk Tunes	*Boosey and Hawkes*
arr Adair	Ducks and Drakes	*Boosey and Hawkes*

Infant Junior

arr Adair	Tunes for Children Sets 1–4	*OUP*
arr Dankworth	Play Tunes	*Feldman/EMI*

Junior

arr Selmer	Five Folk Tunes from Norway	*Chester*
arr Geen	Hunting the Hare	*Feldman/EMI*
arr Mendoza	Three Times Three	*Keith Prowse/EMI*
arr Stephenson	The Classroom orchestra	*Hohner*

CLASSICAL
Junior

arr Hedges	A Rameau Suite	*Chester*
arr Lang	Fitzwilliam Fancies	*Chester*

Junior Secondary

arr Bergese	Music for Orff-Instrumentarium	*Moseler/Novello*
arr Brace	Something to Play	*CUP*
arr Waddington [ ] Benoy	Two Marches of Beethoven	*OUP*
arr Winters	Three Pieces by Jeremiah Clarke	*OUP*

MODERN
Junior

Lorentzen	Six Pieces for Three Instruments	*Chester*
Stone	Diversions	*Boosey and Hawkes*

Junior Secondary

Russell-Smith	A Modern Musical Box	*Belwin Mills*
Steel	Dance – East and West	*Novello*
Stephens	Two Ostinato Pieces	*Chester*
Stone	Pastoral Suite	*Boosey and Hawkes*
Winters	A Cowboy Suite	*Universal*

Secondary

Hand	Carillons	*Novello*

RECORDERS
Descants

Addison	Play and Sing I and II	*Holmes McDougall*
Hand	Come and Play	*OUP*
Kodaly	The Leveret	*Universal*
Salkeld	For the Left Hand	*Schott*
Simpson	Suite on Three Notes	*Schott*
Simpson	Twelve for Two	*Belwin Mills*
Taylor	Recorder Tunes for Beginners	*Faber/Curwen*
arr Appleby/Fowler	Oxford Books of Recorder Music	*OUP*
arr Benoy	Seven Pieces by Classical Composers	*OUP*
arr Clark/Evans	Swing Partners	*Novello*
arr Moragas/Rogers	Spanish Tunes	*Schott*
arr Paviour	Gilbert and Sullivan in Consort	*Belwin Mills*

Recorder and Voices

arr Bergmann	Marching through Georgia	*Schott*
arr Bergmann	Second School Ensemble Book	*Schott*
arr Dinn	Four American Folk Songs	*Lengnick*
arr Goodyear/Payne	Songs and Dances of Scandinavia	*Belwin Mills*
arr Hand	Twelve Unison Songs with Recorder and Piano	*OUP*
Lawrence	Fifty Simple Rounds for Singers and Recorders	*Novello*

Recorder Ensemble

arr Dale	Five Folk Songs	*Feldman/EMI*
arr Dinn	Four Folk Tunes from Europe	*OUP*
arr Dinn	Ten Dovetailed Tunes	*Schott*
arr Hand	Ten German Songs	*OUP*
arr Ring	Renaissance Songs and Dances	*Universal*
Bartok	Peasant Songs and Dances I and II	*Universal*
Bonsor	Three into Five	*Schott*
Chagrin	Album for Nicolas	*Chappell*
Salkeld	First Concert Pieces for Recorder I and II	*Schott*
Taylor	Elementary Duets for Descant and Treble Recorders	*Faber/Curwen*

PENTATONIC TUNES

1 One Two Three Along		
*2 Khasi's Lullaby	Thirty Folk Settings for Children	*Faber/Curwen*
3 Mistress Brown		
4 Jimalong Josie	Oxford School Music Books Beginners I	*OUP*
*5 Sing Said the Mother	Oxford School Music Books Junior I	*OUP*
6 Turn the Glasses Over	Oxford School Music Books Junior I	*OUP*
7 Sourwood Mountain	Oxford School Music Books Junior II	*OUP*
8 Liza Jane	Oxford School Music Books Junior III	*OUP*
*9 Row Your Boat	Singing Games and Songs	*Schott*
10 Shortnin' Bread		*Schott*
11 Missa Ramgoat	Seventy Simple Songs with Ostinato	*Novello*
*12 Grandma Grunts	Music Together	*Longman*
13 Frog Went A-Courtin'	Songs of the New World	*Holmes McDougall*
14 Cedar Swamp	More Songs of the New World	*Holmes McDougall*

*6 notes but the extra note is a 'passing' note

COLLECTIONS OF PENTATONIC SONGS

Brocklehurst	Pentatonic Song Book I and II	*Schott*
Kersey	Just Five I and II	*Belwin Mills*
Orff/Keetman	Music for Children Book I	*Schott*

VOICES AND INSTRUMENTS: MUSIC AND RECORDS

Music   Records

Infant Junior

Feldman............Play Songs.....................................*Audio-Visual Productions*

Feldman............Play Tunes.....................................*Audio-Visual Productions*

Faber/Curwen   Thirty Folk Settings for Children

Songs for Children...........................*Argo DA 32*

Junior

Faber/Curwen   Thirty More Folk Settings
for Children

The World of the Very Young............*Decca Record
SPAA 165
Decca Cassette
KCSP 165*

Junior Secondary

Schott...............Music for Children I and II...............*HMV SLS 815*

RECORDS FOR CHILDREN

Catalogues available from:

Kiddicraft Records, Kiddicraft Ltd, Kenley, Surrey CR2 5YS

Audio-Visual Productions, 15 Temple Sheen Road, London SW14 7PY

BBC, Broadcasting House, Portland Place, London W1A 1AA

Children's Tape Club Series

Music for Pleasure   EMI House, Manchester Square, London W1A 1ES

Classical Records

Argo Records, 115 Fulham Road, London SW3 6RR

Derek Lawson, 287 Kenton Lane, Kenton, Middlesex HA3 8RR. School File

Hamilton's of Teesside, 14–22 Southgate, Wakefield, Yorks WF1 1SF

Acknowledgements

To Dr Percy M. Young and Holmes McDougall Ltd for an extract from 'By the Stream' from A First Garland of Great Tunes No 17